	The Self	Man, woman, the human race
ᛉ	Partnership	A gift, offerings from the gods or from chiefs to loyal followers
ᚠ	Signals	The Norse god Loki, mouth (source of Divine utterances), river mouth
	Separation	Inherited property or possessions, also native land, home
ᚢ	Strength	Strength, sacrificial animal, the aurochs (*bos primigenius*), species of wild ox
	Initiation	Uncertain meaning, a secret matter
	Constraint	Need, necessity, constraint, cause of human sorrow, lessons, hardship
	Fertility	Ing, legendary hero, later a god
	Defense	Yew tree, a bow made of yew, avertive powers, runic calendars or "primstaves"
ᛦ	Protection	Protection, the elk, sedge or eelgrass
ᚨ	Possessions	Cattle, goods, vital community wealth
ᚹ	Joy	Joy, absence of suffering and sorrow (see *Cynewulf*'s runic passages)
◇	Harvest	Year, harvest, a fruitful part of the year
‹	Opening	Torch, skiff, associated with the goddess Nerthus
↑	Warrior	Victory in battle, a guiding planet or star, the Norse god Tiw (whose name survives in Tuesday)
ᛒ	Growth	Birch tree, associated with fertility rites, rebirth, new life
ᛘ	Movement	Horse, associated with the course of the sun
ᚱ	Flow	Water, sea, a fertility source (see Grendel's Mere in *Beowulf*)
ᚺ	Disruption	Hail, sleet, natural forces that damage
ᚱ	Journey	A journey, riding, carriage, refers to the soul after death; a journey charm
ᚦ	Gateway	Giant, demon, a thorn, the Norse god Thor
ᛞ	Breakthrough	Day, God's light, prosperity and fruitfulness
I	Standstill	Ice, freezing, (in the *Prose Edda,* the frost-giant Ymir is born of ice)
ᛋ	Wholeness	The sun
ᚷ	The Unknowable	The Divine in all human transactions

The
BOOK of
RUNES

A Handbook for the Use of
an Ancient Oracle:
The Viking Runes

Tenth Anniversary Edition

Commentary by
Ralph H. Blum

ST. MARTIN'S PRESS
NEW YORK

Edited by Bronwyn Jones
Illustrations by Jancis Salerno

Library of Congress Cataloging-in-Publication Data
Blum, Ralph
    The book of runes / Ralph H. Blum.—10th anniversary ed.
        p.   cm.
    Includes bibliographical references.
    ISBN 0-312-09758-1/set   0-312-10819-2/HC
    1. Runes—Miscellanea.   2. Oracles.   I. Title.
  BF1779.R86B58   1993
  133.3'3—dc20   93-25945
                                                        CIP

10 9 8 7 6 5 4

This book is lovingly dedicated
to
Margaret Mead

*To lend courage to virtue
and ardor to truth . . .*

—Dr. Samuel Johnson

CONTENTS

ACKNOWLEDGMENTS

For my introduction to the study of Oracles, I am indebted to Dr. Allan W. Anderson, formerly of the Department of Religious Studies, San Diego State University. Dr. Anderson taught a remarkable course entitled "The Oracular Tradition" in which he presented the *I Ching* as "the only systematic sacred text we possess." His scholarship, his presentation of seminal concepts, and his creative influence encouraged me to persevere in my study of "the finest art of all—the art of self-change."

I am especially grateful to Murray Hope who, on a bleak and rainy English afternoon, in Redhill, Surrey, introduced me to the Runes as a contemporary Oracle.

My first attempts at writing this handbook for the use of the Runes as a personal Oracle included many additional pages of history, philology, and archeology (see *The RuneCards*, St. Martin's Press). For support and encouragement in reducing the text to this more concise and manageable form, I gratefully thank my friend and editor, Bronwyn Jones.

Finally, my sincere appreciation to Tom Dunne, my editor at St. Martin's Press, who has been unstintingly generous in encouraging me to introduce new insights and techniques into the original text.

PREFACE

The Runes as described here are healing, merciful Runes; they will do you no harm. Learn their language and let them speak to you. Play with the possibility that they can provide "a mirror for the magic of our Knowing Selves," a means of communication with the knowledge of our subconscious minds.

Remember that you are consulting an Oracle rather than having your fortune told. An Oracle does not give you instruction as to what to do next, nor does it predict future events. An Oracle points your attention towards those hidden fears and motivations that will shape your future by their unfelt presence within each present moment. Once seen and recognized, these elements become absorbed into the realm of choice. Oracles do not absolve you of the responsibility for selecting your future, but rather direct your attention towards those inner choices that may be the most important elements in determining that future.

How can the random selection of marked stones tell you anything about yourself? Perhaps these Rune interpretations are simply so evocative that each contains *some* point which can be accepted as relevant to *some* part of what is happening at the limits of consciousness any day, any time, to anyone. That is the easiest possibility to accept from a strictly scientific

8

standpoint. Nevertheless, my own play with these Runes has shown coincidence piled upon coincidence and an apparently consistent "appropriateness" in each Rune reading that is difficult to explain by the mechanism I have just described.

Can there be other factors that distort the expected randomness of Rune selection so as to provide a language by which the subconscious makes itself and its expectations known? For myself, I maintain an open mind, reminding myself that observations should not be discounted simply because their underlying mechanisms have not yet been satisfactorily explained.

So go ahead. Try out these Runes. See if this Oracle can mirror your subconscious process, but remember that such a link may take practice to develop. The Rune interpretations offered in this work come from the meditations of a gentle, healing mind. They will speak to you of change and growth. The only negativity you will find here relates to the blockage of appropriate growth, while all the positive aspects are transcendent, transforming and lead to breakthroughs. The subconscious you will encounter here is not a fearsome beast in need of obedience training. It is the inner seeker-after-truth who must be helped to save us from ourselves.

Dr. Martin D. Rayner
Professor of Physiology
University of Hawaii School of Medicine

Odin on the Yggdrasil,
or World Tree,
Spies the Runes

THE SPEECH OF THE HIGH ONE

I know I hung on that windswept tree,
Swung there for nine long nights,
Wounded by my own blade,
Bloodied for Odin,
Myself an offering to myself:
Bound to the tree
That no man knows
Whither the roots of it run.

None gave me bread,
None gave me drink.
Down to the deepest depths I peered
Until I spied the Runes.
With a roaring cry I seized them up,
Then dizzy and fainting, I fell.

Well-being I won
And wisdom too.
I grew and took joy in my growth:
From a word to a word
I was led to a word,
From a deed to another deed.

—The Poetic Edda (ca. A.D. 1200)

INTRODUCTION

Few people today have even heard the word "Runes." Among those of Scandinavian descent, those who enjoy crossword puzzles and among readers of J.R.R. Tolkien, yes, a light goes on. But that's about the extent of it. An ancient alphabetic script, each of whose letters possessed a meaningful name as well as a signifying sound, Runes were employed for legal documents, for writing poetry, for inscriptions and divination, yet never evolved as a spoken language.

Both the alphabetical ordering and the letter interpretations found in *The Book of Runes* are nonconventional. The original interpretations of the Runes are lost to us. While *legomonism*—the passing on of sacred knowledge through initiation—was practiced among Rune casters of old, their secrets were not recorded or, if recorded, did not survive. In ancient times, the Runes and their symbols were employed by warriors bent on conquest. It is my hope that the Runes, in their contemporary use, will serve the Spiritual Warrior, the one whose quest is doing battle with the self, the one whose goal is self-change. The sacred Hindu text, the *Bhagavad Gita*, says it well in Chapter 6, verse 5:

> *Lift up the self by the Self*
> *And don't let the self droop down,*

*For the Self is the self's only friend
And the self is the Self's only foe.**

The Book of Runes is offered as a handbook for the Spiritual Warrior. Free of anxiety, radically alone and unattached to outcomes, the Spiritual Warrior practices absolute trust in the struggle for awareness, and is constantly mindful that what matters is to have a *true present*. It takes a long time to grow in wisdom, to say nothing of the time it takes to learn to think well. Following the way of the Spiritual Warrior is not for everyone, although it is available to all who are willing to undergo its challenges. To embark on such a path is to cultivate the Witness Self, the Watcher Within, the One who can profitably converse through the Runes.

Before beginning to write this book, I consulted the Runes on the timeliness of the undertaking. The three Runes I drew were *Inguz* ◊, the Rune of Fertility and New Beginnings; *Nauthiz* ᚾ, the Rune of Constraint, Necessity and Pain; and *Dagaz* ᛞ, the Rune of Breakthrough and Transformation. The interpretations of the twenty-five Runes were conceived in one fertile sleepless night. The long hours spent in finding the form, editing and reworking the first half of the book, were certainly not without pain. Yet through it all, I remained mindful of the French saying: "Pain is the craft entering into the apprentice."

*Throughout *The Book of Runes* the term *self* is used to represent the little self or ego-self, and *Self* to signify the Higher Self, the Divine Within.

Working with the Runes has been a source of transformation in my life and, through their introduction to the Runes, the lives of many others.

All along the way there have been positive signs and omens. The final sign came as I completed the Afterword. Since the last Rune masters lived in seventeenth-century Iceland, it seemed to me fitting to close with an Icelandic blessing. In order to check the spelling of *Gud blessi thig*, the Icelandic for "God bless you," I placed a call to the Icelandic Consulate in New York. The woman who answered confirmed the spelling. When I told her about my work, she paused a long moment, then said, "My name is Sigrun. It means *Rune of Victory*."

* * *

It may seem odd to mark the tenth anniversary of an oracular system that is, in fact, at least two thousand years old. When I first published *The Book of Runes*, I showed it to Buckminster Fuller who squinted at me and remarked, "No easy task—to midwife the return of an ancient Oracle."

As *The Book of Runes* observes, "Function determines form, use confers meaning, and an Oracle always responds to the requirements of the time in which it is consulted." And, I would add, to the needs of those consulting it.

It is my firm conviction that the Runes, as adapted here for the contemporary Rune caster, are not meant to be used for divination or fortune telling.

The disposition of the future is in God's hands, not ours. Rather, the Runes are a tool for assisting us to guide our lives in the *present*. For it is only in the present that our power can be exercised. Think about it—when did you last make a mistake in the future?

The Runes are an instrument for learning the will of the Divine in our lives, a means of listening to that part of ourselves that knows everything we need to know for our lives now. As a method of guidance and self-counseling, the Runes assist us to navigate unfamiliar waters when the old charts no longer serve and we are required to be our own cartographers. A friend put it succinctly when he described the Runes as "a compass for conduct."

Here, then, is a tool for keeping us on course, on track. But first and foremost, the Runes are a training device for strengthening the intuition which is, I suggest, everybody's second language.

Finally, a note on the life of the text of this book. *The Book of Runes* has undergone so many edits—both partial and complete—that my editor, Bronwyn Jones, and I have lost count. At first, I thought I was simply being meticulous in the revisions. But after half a dozen edits of a book already in print for many years, I began to think that I was actually being obsessive. Now, however, I am at peace with the practice of revising and grateful to recognize that process as one of the gifts from the Oracle.

Working with the Runes over the past decade has revealed nuances of interpretation and application that have demanded subtle (and sometimes not so subtle) modifications in the text itself. And that includes the Rune interpretations, where the shift of a phrase or the sharpening of an image has made meaning more accessible, thereby facilitating the use of the Oracle.

So while this Tenth Anniversary Edition does not contain new chapters or new runic practices, it has nevertheless been "made new" both through our deepening understanding of the Oracle, and through thousands of letters from people sharing with us their experiences with the Runes. Thank you all for taking part in midwifing the return of this ancient Oracle.

May the Runes continue to serve you well.

INVOCATION

God within me, God without,
How shall I ever be in doubt?
There is no place where I may go
And not there see God's face, not know
I am God's vision and God's ears.
So through the harvest of my years
I am the Sower and the Sown,
God's Self unfolding and God's own.

Rune stone, Västerby, Uppland, Sweden,
work of Asmund Karasun, *ca.* A.D. 1050

I

THE ORACLE
OF THE SELF

A King he was on a carven throne
In many-pillared halls of stone
With golden roof and silver floor,
And runes of power upon the door.

—J.R.R. Tolkien
The Fellowship of the Ring

Runes and charms are very practical formulae designed to pro-
duce definite results, such as getting a cow out of a bog.

—T. S. Eliot
The Music of Poetry

The purpose of this book is to reintroduce an ancient Oracle, the Runes. Older than the New
Testament, the Runes have lain fallow for more than
400 years. Akin in function to the Tarot and the
Chinese *Book of Changes*, the Runes were last in cur-
rent use in Iceland during the late Middle Ages.

The wisdom of the Rune masters died with them.
Little remains but the standing Rune stones, the sagas,
the far-flung fragments of runic lore and the Runes

19

themselves. In his fine book, *Runes: An Introduction*, Ralph W. V. Elliott writes of

> strange symbols scratched into ancient tools and weapons now lying idle in some museum showcase; names of warriors, secret spells, even snatches of songs, appearing on objects as diverse as minute silver coins and towering stone crosses, scattered in the unlikeliest places from Yugoslavia to Orkney, from Greenland to Greece.*

The influence of the Runes on their time is incontestable. Elliott notes that when the high chieftains and wise counselors of Anglo-Saxon England met in conclave, they called their secret deliberations "Runes," and that when Bishop Wulfila made his translation of the Bible into fourth-century Gothic, he rendered St. Mark's "the mystery of the kingdom of God" (Mark 4:11) using *runa* for "mystery." Eight centuries earlier, when the Greek historian Herodotus traveled around the Black Sea, he encountered descendants of Scythian tribesmen who crawled under blankets, smoked themselves into a stupor (a practice still encountered even today in the Caucasus Mountains) and then cast marked sticks in the air and "read" them when they fell. Although these tribesmen were preliterate, their sticks would probably qualify as *runakefli* or Rune sticks.

There is no firm agreement among scholars as to

*Ralph W. V. Elliott, *Runes: An Introduction* (Manchester, Eng.: Manchester University Press, 1959), p. 1.

where and when runic writing first made its appearance in Western Europe.* Before the Germanic peoples possessed any form of script, they used pictorial symbols that they scratched onto rocks. Especially common in Sweden, these prehistoric rock carvings or *hällristningar* are dated from the second Bronze Age (*ca.* 1300 B.C.), and were probably linked to Indo-European fertility and sun cults. The carvings include representations of men and animals, parts of the human body, weapon motifs, sun symbols, the swastika and variations on square and circular forms:

⊗ ✳ ◎ ⅄ ＋ ⊞ 目 ⋔ ⅄

↗ ↑ ⚎ ⅄ ⅄ ⅄ ⌀ ⅄ Ψ

Elliott suggests an amalgamation of two separate traditions, "the alphabetic script on the one hand, the symbolic content on the other. . . . The practice of sortilege (divination) was cultivated among Northern Italic as well as Germanic peoples, the one using letters, the others pictorial symbols."† Numerous *hällristningar*, as well as the runic standing stones, can still be seen in the British Isles, in Germany and throughout Scandinavia.

It is difficult for us to imagine the immense pow-

---

*Elliott writes: "All we know then is that in some Germanic tribe some man had both the leisure (a factor often forgotten) and the remarkable phonetic sense to catch the *futhark* (alphabetic script) from a North Italic model known to him somewhere in the alpine regions in the period c. 250–150 B.C." Op. cit., p. 11.

†Elliott, op. cit., pp. 64–5.

ers bestowed on the few who became skilled in the use of symbolic markings or glyphs to convey meaning. Those first glyphs were called *runes*, from the Gothic *runa*, meaning "a secret thing, a mystery." The runic letter, or *runastafr*, became a repository for intuitions that were enriched according to the skill of the practitioner of *runemal*, the art of Rune casting.

From the beginning, the Runes took on a ritual function, serving for the casting of lots, for divination and to evoke higher powers that could influence the lives and fortunes of the people. The craft of *runemal* touched every aspect of life, from the most sacred to the most practical. There were Runes and spells to influence the weather, the tides, crops, love, healing; Runes of fertility, cursing and removing curses, birth and death. Runes were carved on amulets, drinking cups, battle spears, over the lintels of dwellings and onto the prows of Viking ships.

The Rune casters of the Teutons and Vikings wore startling garb that made them easily recognizable. Honored, welcomed, feared, these shamans were familiar figures in tribal circles. There is evidence that a fair number of runic practitioners were women. The anonymous author of the thirteenth-century *Saga of Erik the Red* provides a vivid description of a contemporary mistress of runecraft:

> She wore a cloak set with stones along the hem. Around her neck and covering her head she wore a hood lined with white catskins. In one hand, she

carried a staff with a knob on the end and at her belt, holding together her long dress, hung a charm pouch.

To pre-Christian eyes, the earth and all created things were alive. Twigs and stones served for Runecasting since, as natural objects, they were believed to embody the sacred. Runic symbols were carved into pieces of hardwood, incised on metal or cut into leather that was then stained with pigment into which human blood was sometimes mixed to enhance the potency of the spell. The most common Runes were smooth flat pebbles with symbols or glyphs painted on one side. The practitioners of *runemal* would shake their pouch and scatter the pebbles on the ground; those falling with glyphs upward were then interpreted.

The most explicit surviving description of this procedure comes from the Roman historian Tacitus. Writing in A.D. 98 about practices prevalent among the Germanic tribes, he reports:

To divination and casting of lots they pay attention beyond any other people. Their method of casting lots is a simple one: they cut a branch from a fruit-bearing tree and divide it into small pieces which they mark with certain distinctive signs *(notae)* and scatter at random onto a white cloth. Then, the priest of the community, if the lots are consulted publicly, or the father of the family, if it is done privately, after invoking the gods and with eyes raised to heaven, picks up three pieces, one at a time, and interprets them according to the signs previously marked upon them.

(Germania, Ch. X)

By Tacitus' time, the Runes were already becoming widely known on the Continent. They were carried from place to place by traders, adventurers and warriors and, eventually, by Anglo-Saxon missionaries. For this dispersion to occur, a common alphabet was required, the alphabet that became known as *futhark* after its first six letters:

Although later Anglo-Saxon alphabets expanded to include as many as thirty-three letters in Britain, the traditional Germanic futhark is comprised of twenty-four Runes. These were divided into three "families" of eight Runes each, three and eight being numbers credited with special potency. The three groups, known as *aettir*, were named for the Norse gods *Freyr*, *Hagal* and *Tyr*. The three *aettir* are:

It is with these twenty-four Runes, plus one later innovation—the Blank Rune, the Rune that stands for the Unknowable, for the presence of the Divine in all transactions—that *The Book of Runes* is concerned.

THE RUNE OF HOSPITALITY

I saw a stranger yestereen;
I put food in the eating place,
*   Drink in the drinking place,*
*   Music in the listening place;*
And in the sacred names of the Triune
He blessed me and my house,
*   My cattle and my dear ones.*
And the lark said in her song:
*   Often, often, often,*
Goes the Christ in the stranger's guise.
*   Often, often, often,*
Goes the Christ in the stranger's guise.

—From the Gaelic

Christ figure, Jaellinge, Denmark, *ca.* A.D. 980

2

THE EMERGENCE
OF THE RUNES

oracle, *from the Latin oraculum, divine announcement . . .*
1. among the ancient Greeks and Romans, a) the place where,
or medium by which, deities were consulted; b) the revelation
or response of a medium or priest; 2. a) any person or agency
believed to be in communication with a deity; b) any person of
great knowledge or wisdom; c) opinions or statements of any
such oracle; 3) the holy of holies of the ancient Jewish Temple.

—Webster's New World Dictionary

And the oracle he prepared in the house within, to set there the
ark of the convenant of the Lord.

—I Kings 6:19

When I began to work with the Runes, I had
never seen a runic text and, therefore, did not realize
that I was breaking away from the traditional sequence of Freyr, Hagal and Tyr used by the early
practitioners of *runemal*. But function determines
form, use confers meaning and an Oracle always responds to the requirements of the time in which it is
consulted—and to the needs of those consulting it. In

the end I relied on the Runes to establish their own order and to instruct me in their meanings.

The Rune stones I was working with had come to me in England: tiny brown rectangles hardly bigger than a thumbnail, with the glyphs scratched onto their surfaces. The woman who made them lived on Trindles Road, in the town of Redhill, Surrey. She hadn't glazed her Runes, merely baked them in her oven like cookies.

Along with this set of Runes came two unnumbered Xeroxed sheets giving the glyphs, their approximate English meanings, and a brief interpretation for each Rune when "Upright" or "Reversed." To the twenty-four original *futhark* Runes had been added a Blank Rune defined as "The path of karma; that which is predestined and cannot be avoided. Matters hidden by the gods." There were no instructions for using the Runes and, after a few days, the Trindles Road Runes went into a suitcase.

Almost a year passed before I happened upon them again. Alone on my Connecticut farm on a warm summer evening, unable to sleep, I went to my study and began rearranging books. And there, in their little chamois bag, were the Runes.

As I spilled the stones out onto my desk and moved them around, I experienced the same pleasurable feeling as when I first handled them in England. And yet I didn't really know how to use the Oracle. It was then that it occurred to me to ask the Runes how they were to be consulted. I sat quietly for a time, composing myself, then said a prayer. I opened my notebook and wrote out this question: "In what order do you wish to be arranged?"

I spread out the Runes on my desk, blank sides up, and moved them around, touching each stone. Then, one by one, I turned them over, aligning them in front of me in three rows. It took only a few moments. When I was done, I sat and studied the arrangement:

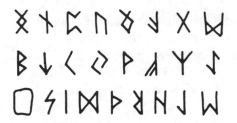

I remember my first feeling of dismay that The Blank Rune, The Unknowable, had not positioned itself more dramatically, rather than simply taking its place among the rest. And then I got an eerie feeling: I had been told that the Runes could be read *from right to left*.* Seen that way, the sequence began with the Rune of The Self, *Mannaz* , and ended with The

---

*Traditionally, the Runes could face either way and be read from left or right or, on occasion, vertically. Some inscriptions were laid out and read *boustrophedon*—from the Greek *bous*, an ox, and *strophe*, to turn— meaning the way an ox travels when plowing. See illustration on p. **36.**

Blank Rune, the Rune that signals the presence of the Divine in our lives. In other words, here was an alphabet that was at the same time *a map for the self on its journey back to its Source.*

I picked up *Mannaz* [ᛗ], the Rune of The Self. While I sat gazing at it, these words came to me:

> *The starting point is the self. It's essence is water. Only clarity, willingness to change, is effective now. A correct relationship to yourself is primary, for from it flow all possible right relationships with others and with the Divine.*

The Viking Runes had begun their teaching.

I worked on through the night, taking each Rune in my hand, sitting with it, meditating on its essential meaning, writing down what came to me. Now and then, when the flow dwindled, I turned to the ancient Chinese oracular system, the *I Ching*, and asked for a hexagram that would reveal the character of a particular Rune. The spirit of some of those readings is incorporated into the interpretations of the Viking Runes. By the time I had completed the interpretation of The Blank Rune, the sun was rising. The time was 6:31 A.M., and the date was June 22. Without realizing it, I had worked through the night of the Summer Solstice.

Since that night, I have read a great deal about the Runes and their history, the controversies over their origins, the speculations concerning their use. Only one thing is certain: Beyond all the efforts of scholars to encompass them, the Runes remain elusive, for they are Odin's gift, and sacred.

THE GIFT OF ODIN

Odin is the principal divinity in the pantheon of Norse gods. His name derives from the Old Norse for "wind" and "spirit." It was his passion, his transforming sacrifice of the self, that brought the Runes to humankind. According to legend, Odin hung for nine nights on *Yggdrasil*, the Tree of the World, wounded by his own blade, tormented by hunger, thirst and pain, unaided and alone until, before he fell, he spied the Runes and, with a last tremendous effort, seized them.

Next to the gift of fire, that of the alphabet is the light in which we see our nature revealed. In the Old Norse poem, *The Poetic Edda*, Odin, the great Rune Master, speaks across the centuries. Hear Odin now:

> *Do you know how to cut them,*
> *   know how to stain them,*
> *Know how to read them,*
> *   how to understand?*
> *Do you know how to evoke them,*
> *   know how to send them,*
> *Know how to offer, know how to ask?*

> *It is better not to offer than to offer too much*
> *   for a gift demands a gift.*
> *Better not to slay than to slay too many.*
> *Thus did Odin speak before the earth began*
> *   when he rose up in after time.*

These runes I know, unknown to kings' wives
Or any earthly man. "Help" one is called,
For help is its gift, and helped you will be
In sickness and care and sorrow.

Another I know, which all will need
Who would study leechcraft.
On the bark scratch them, on the bole of trees
Whose boughs bend to the east.

I know a third:
If my need be great in battle
It dulls the swords of deadly foes,
Neither wiles nor weapons wound me
And I go all unscathed . . .

The motto for the Runes could be the same words that were carved above the gate of the Oracle at Delphi: *Know thyself.* The Runes are a teacher and a source of guidance. Consider this Oracle, if you will, as a sacred game, an instrument for serious or high play. For the value of play is that it frees us from the effort of learning, frees us to learn as children learn.

The truth is that each of us is an Oracle, and when we pray we are exercising our true oracular function, which is to address the Knowing Self within. Consulting the Runes will put you in touch with your own inner guidance, with that part of you that knows everything you need to know for your life now.

One prominent modern authority for the efficacy of Oracles is the Swiss psychiatrist Carl Jung. Jung affirmed that "theoretical considerations of cause and effect often look pale and dusty in comparison to the practical results of chance."* This suggests that nothing is too insignificant to be regarded as a clue to guide us in right and timely action. Consulting an Oracle places you in true present time because whatever happens in the given moment possesses what Jung calls "the quality peculiar to that moment."

Experiencing a *true present* is something most of us find extremely difficult. We waste a good part of our lives dwelling on past regrets and fantasies of the future. In my own life, when I jog or drive long distances, I find I am often busy reviewing ideas, sorting agendas, going over options and possibilities. Then I catch myself: I realize that miles of countryside have slipped by unseen, that I am not aware of breathing the air, not aware of the trees, the breeze, the contours and colors of the land.

Nowadays, I catch myself more and more frequently, which is a start. The "roof-brain chatter" is slowly being replaced with a stillness that keeps me in the present. Once the momentum is broken, the habit will soon wither. We have only to remember: *In the spiritual life, we are always at the beginning.* Remembering

---

*C. G. Jung, Foreword to the *I Ching* (Princeton, N.J.: Princeton University Press, 1950).

this helps us to overcome our addiction to "getting ahead." For when we experience a true present, that is where everything happens.

Consulting the Runes enables you to bypass the strictures of reason, the fetters of conditioning and the momentum of habit.* For the brief span of interacting with the Oracle, you are declaring a free zone in which your life is malleable, vulnerable, open to change.

We are living in an age of radical discontinuity. The lessons come faster and faster as our souls and the universe push us into new growth. Familiar waters seem suddenly perilous, alive with uncharted shoals and shifting sandbars. The old maps are outdated; we require new navigational aids. And the inescapable fact is: *You are your own cartographer now.* Just as the Vikings used the information provided by the Rune masters to navigate and sail their ships under cloudy skies, so now you can employ the Runes to modify your own life course. A shift of a few degrees at the beginning of any voyage will mean a vastly different position far out to sea.

Whatever the Runes may be—a bridge between the self and Self, a link between the Self and the Divine, an ageless navigational aid—the energy that engages them is our own and, ultimately, the wisdom

---

*As Brugh Joy reminds us in his useful guidebook, *Joy's Way: A Map for the Transitional Journey,* there are three sets of mental fetters to give up if you want to be truly free: judging, comparing and needing to know why.

as well. Thus, as we start to make contact with our Knowing Selves, we will begin to hear messages of profound beauty and true usefulness. For like snow-flakes and fingerprints, each of our oracular signa-tures is a one-of-a-kind aspect of Creation addressing its own.

CREDO

The truth is that life is hard and dangerous; that those who seek their own happiness do not find it; that those who are weak must suffer; that those who demand love will be disappointed; that those who are greedy will not be fed; that those who seek peace will find strife; that truth is only for the brave; that joy is only for those who do not fear to be alone; that life is only for the one who is not afraid to die.

—Joyce Cary

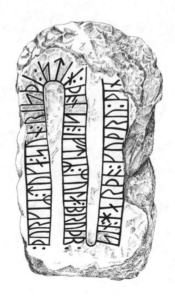

Boustrophedon script on stone
near Asferg, Sweden

3

CONSULTING
THE ORACLE

The real voyage of discovery consists not in seeking new landscapes but in having new eyes.

—Marcel Proust

Lord, grant me weak eyes for things that are of no account and strong eyes for all Thy truth.

—Søren Kierkegaard

We walk by faith and not by sight.

—St. Paul

Once you start exploring the world of Runes, you will discover that many people have developed their own forms of personal Rune casting. There was an old man who worked the boardwalk in Venice, California. He sat on a sheet on which he had painted the rainbow circles of a bull's-eye. He had a bag of stones, shells and twigs, and when you posed your question he scattered his "Runes" and read from their spread. There are people who make Runes out of sand dollars, bits of bone or stones upon which they carve their own symbols. The possibilities and permutations are endless.

Then there is what some people call "Noah Webster's Oracle." You open the dictionary at random, place your finger anywhere on the page, and take your counsel from the words beneath your finger. At one moment, while working intensively on this book, I was presented with an attractive business opportunity that I felt obliged to pass up. And yet, by doing so, I feared I might be missing out. I began giving myself a hard time. Instead of consulting the Runes on this issue, I opened a dictionary and, without looking, set my finger on the page. The counsel I received came under the words *lay off*, and contained the phrases "mark off boundaries . . . stop criticizing . . . minimize risk." I returned to the manuscript with a clear conscience.

Over the years, I have met a number of people who, without any precise knowledge of Oracles, employed the Bible in a similar fashion. It has long been my habit to consult the *Daily Word** and attempt to live by its wisdom. It is a teacher for me, a monthly source of daily Oracles.

Such contemporary Oracles, however homespun, are consistent with ancient traditions—such as the Chinese practice of reading Oracle bones or cracks that appear on tortoise shells when heated in a fire—and with the practice of *runemal* itself.

*An excellent collection of daily inspirational readings published by Unity, Unity Village, Missouri 64065.

While working with the Runes, I have considered what, at its most basic, constitutes a Rune. At what point is special meaning present in a sign or glyph? Have you noticed the Warrior Rune ⊖ on highways? Or the Rune of Opening ⟨ ... ⟨ ... in a series at sharp curves? Meaning is clearly present, agreed upon, but hardly oracular in nature—unless, of course, you happen to be mulling over an issue, see the sign at that moment, and it holds a personal message for you.

While I was working on this book in California, I had a curious runic encounter. One afternoon, driving to the beach to give a counseling session, I took the Las Virgines-Malibu Canyon Road, a beautiful drive through the mountains. Coming out of a curve, I looked across the canyon and there, on the mountain-side opposite, someone had painted a Rune the height of a man. No question about it—I was looking up at *Algiz* ↑ , the Rune of Protection. The glyph was painted on the rock face Reversed, a call for caution in the runic vocabulary.

Unsolicited but nevertheless appropriate, this runic communication counseled me to set proper boundaries with my client, a powerful film producer who expected me to drop whatever I was doing and attend to his needs. The artist had enclosed the Rune in a circle so that it appeared like this ⊕. It took me a moment to realize that what I was seeing was a rallying symbol from the antiwar movement of the 1960s. How curious that, probably without ever realizing it, the protesters had adopted the Rune of Protection. I drove on, wondering whether, centuries from now, some zealous graduate student would attempt to prove that the ancient Vikings had actually made it all the way to Malibu.

CONSULTING THE RUNES

There are people who simply set aside a time each day at which to cast the Runes. Others prefer a more formal approach: lighting a candle, perhaps a stick of incense, taking time to compose themselves. Some find that meditation on the breath is helpful: Follow the breath in and out; let the breaths be long, easy, connected. Release all cares and concerns, if only for a moment. You may wish to say a prayer, especially if the situation confronting you is intense or turbulent.

Focus is important. But even if the ordinary business of living intrudes, you can always consult the Runes without formal preparation. Your need is what brings the energy of the Runes into play. And remember, you *are* in the realm of play, sacred play. A particularly good time to consult the Runes is when you have exhausted your own resources and are facing a situation about which you possess limited or incomplete information. Focus the issue clearly in your mind,* reach

---

*"Just as in interpreting a dream, one must follow the dream text with utmost exactitude, so in consulting the oracle, one must hold in mind the form of the question put, for this sets a definite limit to the interpretation of the answer." C. G. Jung, op.cit., p. xxxvi.

into your bag, make contact with the stones and draw a Rune. As one practitioner of *runemal* put it, "The right Rune always sticks to my fingers."

When you cast the Runes for someone else, ask the person to formulate the matter of concern clearly in their mind but *not* state it aloud. This eliminates any unconscious personal bias in your interpretation.

If a friend who lives far away could benefit from the perspective of a Rune reading, the telephone is your ally. Ask your friend to focus on their issue, then draw a Rune from your bag. A Rune reading is as effective across 8,000 miles as when it is done face to face.

Should you wish to consult the Runes for another person and cannot ask their permission directly, it is best to inquire of the Oracle whether such action is timely and correct. Ask for a "Yes" or a "No" by reaching into your bag and drawing a Rune. Upright is "Yes," Reversed, "No." If you happen to draw one of the nine Runes that read the same Upright and Reversed, draw again.

APPROPRIATE ISSUES

An appropriate issue is *anything that relates to timeliness and right action.* You might require advice on whether or not to make a career change, sell a business, make an investment, move to a new home, terminate or initiate a relationship.

Notice that the word *issue* is used rather than *question*. A question might be, "Should I end this relationship?" To state the matter as an issue, you would say, "The issue is my relationship." Instead of asking, "Should I accept this new job?" you might say, "The issue is my work." This small distinction is crucial. If you ask a question and the Oracle provides the answer, then your role is a passive one. However, if you address an issue, and the Oracle comments on that issue, this allows you to extract your own answer and determine for yourself what is right action.

If you don't have a specific issue in mind, and still you feel drawn to consult the Runes, simply ask: *What do I need to know for my life now?* The Oracle's reply will always be timely and instructive.

RUNIC OVERRIDE

Occasionally you may find that the counsel you receive doesn't apply to your issue. When this occurs, consider the possibility that the Runes are addressing a more significant or more timely issue, something you are avoiding, or something of which you are not consciously aware. This *runic override* seems to be an automatic fail-safe device. Similarly, if you find yourself caught between two issues and can't decide which one to address, don't worry, the Runes—which is to say your own Inner Knowing—will select for you by addressing the issue of most immediate concern.

UPRIGHT AND REVERSED READINGS

Nine of the Runes read the same regardless of how you draw them from the bag. The other sixteen can be read either Upright or Reversed.

For example, the Rune of Movement, *Ehwaz*, Upright, looks like this: [M], and Reversed, like this: [W]. The Reversed reading draws attention to aspects of a situation that might impede movement, or to the fact that movement itself might be inappropriate at this time.

It is well to remember that drawing a Reversed Rune is not a cause for alarm but rather an indication that care and attention are required for your conduct to be correct. A Reversed reading often signals an opportunity to challenge some aspect of your behavior, some area in your life which, until now, you have been unwilling to face.

Whether you draw your Rune Upright or Reversed, it is always a good idea to read *both* interpretations. Doing so will put you in touch with all aspects of the situation, including that which is not currently being expressed.

CONSULTING TWO ORACLES

When you first start using the Runes, you may want to check them for accuracy. This can be done by consulting two oracular instruments on the same issue.

When I began working with the Runes, in order to confirm the Oracle's responses with those of a known and wise friend, I would often pose the same issue both to the *I Ching* and to the Runes. Time after time, I found the two Oracles to be in accord, sometimes identical in their symbolic content, often complementary, always a mutual enrichment.

MAKING YOUR OWN RUNES

You may wish to create your own set of Runes. Runes have been cut out of wood with the glyphs burned onto them. A Navajo silversmith in Santa Fe, New Mexico, once crafted a particularly lovely set for me. Flat pebbles smoothed by the sea or a river make beautiful Runes. Runes can be made from quartz crystal, amethyst, jade, or pieces of bone. I have even, on occasion, created an instant set from shirt cardboard, and inked the glyphs onto the cardboard rectangles with a felt-tipped pen.

The first set of Runes I commissioned was made of clay, twice glazed, by potter Norman Aufrichtig of Brookfield, Connecticut. While making the set, he kept a daub of clay from each stone and then formed The Blank Rune from these daubs. Thus The Blank Rune contained the essence of all life's elements.

If you make your own Runes, or make sets for others, let the doing be a meditation. The idea of meditating is a block for some people—including myself. I finally broke free from my anxiety about not being able to meditate conventionally when I heard mythologist Joseph Campbell say that underlining sentences in books was his meditation. Weeding the garden can be a meditation. So can washing your car. Making your own Runes can be a profound and satisfying meditation.

LENDING YOUR RUNES

Finally, there remains the question of whether or not to lend your Runes to others. Some people will feel comfortable in lending them, others may not. Lending your Runes is a personal matter. For me, the Runes are simply a means of communication. I am comfortable sharing my Runes. When in doubt, simply ask by drawing a Rune from the bag: Upright means "Yes," Reversed means "No." And remember, if you happen to draw one of the Runes that reads the same Upright and Reversed, draw again.

Bridal song written in Runes, eleventh century

THE GREAT INVOCATION

From the point of Light within the mind of God
  Let Light stream forth into the minds of all.
  Let Light descend on Earth.

From the point of Love within the Heart of God
  Let Love stream forth into the hearts of all.
    May Christ return to Earth.

From the center where the Will of God is known
  Let purpose guide our little wills—
    The purpose which the Masters know
      and serve.

From the center which we call the human race
  Let the Plan of Love and Light work out
    And may it seal the door where evil
      dwells.

Let Light and Love and Power
  Restore the Plan on Earth.

—Alice Bailey

RUNEMAL: THE ART OF RUNE CASTING

Remember, you cannot abandon what you do not know. To go beyond yourself, you must know yourself.

—Sri Nisargadatta Maharaj

Like many games, sacred and secular, the Runes are meant to be played upon a field. The field represents the world that is always coming to be and passing away. You may want to use a special piece of fabric, colored or white, that you keep for this purpose alone. When you unfold the cloth that serves as your field, that very act can become a silent meditation. My field, a rainbow weaving created by Patrick Shepherd, once a weaver of the Findhorn Community in Scotland, measures 14 inches by 18 inches and is woven from twenty-two graded hues of silk thread.

My first bag was a found object: purple with a legend stitched on one side announcing that the bag's original contents had been a bottle of Crown Royal whiskey. Someone else drank the whiskey; I inherited the bag. There is something very satisfying about reaching into a bag and choosing a Rune. I like feeling the stones click against each other and, even more, I appreciate the way a Rune often seems to insert itself between my fingers.

But neither bag nor field needs to be ornate: As the *I Ching* reminds us, "Even with slender means, the sentiments of the heart can be expressed."

In ancient times, the Rune caster would chant an invocation to Odin—requesting that the god be present—and then scatter the stones onto the earth, taking counsel from those that fell glyph-side up. If this venerable method seems unwieldy to you, a number of other satisfactory techniques recommend themselves.

ODIN'S RUNE

This is the most practical and simple use of the Oracle and consists of drawing one Rune for an overview of an entire situation. Doing so can help you to focus more clearly on your issue and provide you with a fresh perspective. What you are, in effect, doing is inviting the mind to function intuitively, by invoking the wisdom of the Knowing Self.

Drawing a single Rune is particularly helpful under stressful conditions. You may find yourself dealing with matters that demand action now, and the truth is *you don't have enough information*. To reach a decision, all you require is your bag of Runes and, if possible, a quiet place.

A senior corporate officer once told me that he had suddenly been confronted with a crisis which amounted to taking over his company or resigning. "I headed for the men's room clutching my bag of Runes," he said. "When I came out, I was on my way to becoming the Chief Executive Officer." The Rune he had drawn was *Dagaz* ⋈, the Rune of Breakthrough and Transformation.

Drawing a single Rune is not only valuable in a time of crisis. This technique is useful whenever you require an overview of any situation. On a long drive or commute between home and work, some people keep their Runes beside them on the seat. Drawing Odin's Rune often reveals the humor in a difficult matter. And why not? God's favorite music is laughter.

If you are concerned about someone who is far away and you are unable to contact that person, focus directly on the individual, and then draw a Rune. This practice opens a doorway in the mind to the nonordinary. You may discover that it is indeed possible to know things at a distance, and that your true vision extends as far as the mind can see.

Use the single Rune drawing to honor significant events in your life: birthdays, the New Year, solstices and equinoxes, the death of a friend, births, anniversaries, and other special occasions. You may want to record these castings in a Rune Journal (see page 65).

THREE RUNE SPREAD

The number "three" figures prominently in the oracular practices of the ancients. The *Three Rune Spread* which, according to Tacitus, was already in use 2,000 years ago, is satisfactory for all but the most demanding situations.

With an issue clearly in mind, select three Runes one at a time, and place them from *right to left*, in order of selection.* To avoid consciously changing the direction of the stones, especially as you become familiar with their symbols, you may want to place them blank side up, and then turn them over.

Once you have selected the Runes, they will lie before you in this fashion: Reading from the right, the first Rune provides the *Overview of the Situation*; the second Rune (center) identifies the *Challenge*; and the third Rune (on the left) indicates the *Course of Action Called For*.

How you happen to turn the stones may still alter the direction of the glyphs to either an Upright or

* I prefer to mark down on a sheet of paper the Rune chosen, and then replace the stone in the bag. That way I draw each time from all twenty-five stones. This same option applies to all spreads in this Chapter and in Chapter 5, except where otherwise indicated.

Reversed position, but this too is part of the process. Since only nine Runes read the same Upright and Reversed, the readings for the other sixteen will depend on how you place or turn the stones.

A Sample Reading

A friend came to me for a Rune reading after his wife had left him. He was experiencing a great deal of pain, realizing how much the relationship meant to him and agonizing over his loss. His issue was, "What am I to learn from this separation?" These are the Runes he drew:

The three Runes were interpreted in the following manner: Reading from the right, the first Rune, *Algiz* ⟨⟩, the Rune of Protection *Reversed*, addresses his sense of being totally vulnerable, unprotected. It is a counsel to be mindful that only right action and correct conduct provide protection at such a time. He must learn and grow from this loss. The second Rune, *Kano* ⟨⟩, is the Rune of Opening. He is encouraged to trust his process and consider what aspects of his old conditioning must change. Third came *Nauthiz* ⟨⟩, the Rune of Constraint and Pain. The new growth will not be free of anguish. And yet his wife's departure prompted him to undertake serious work on himself.

He is asked to be mindful, moreover, that rectification must come before progress.

To sum up, the three Runes are saying that, although he is feeling vulnerable and exposed, with pain comes the necessary clarity to get on with the work of self-change. As he progresses, he is reminded to consider the positive uses of adversity.

FIVE RUNE SPREAD

Drawing a single Rune—Odin's Rune—will, as a rule, provide sufficient information to enable you to proceed with right action and skillful means. And yet situations will sometimes arise when the need-to-know extends beyond the authority of a single stone or even a Three Rune Spread. Employing the *Five Rune Spread* can help to identify the distinctive features of a situation that might otherwise overwhelm you with its complexity.

Begin by clearly formulating your issue. Then draw five stones from the bag, one at a time, and place them one below the other. In descending order, let the Runes stand for the following:

(1) *Overview of the Situation*
(2) *Challenge*
(3) *Course of Action Called for*
(4) *Sacrifice*
(5) *New Situation Evolving*

If you select five Runes, and place them one below the other in front of you, the odds against drawing this particular spread are 607,614 to 1. If, however, you decide to mark down the Rune you select and then return it to the bag, you will be making each selection from a full set of Runes, and the odds against drawing this particular spread soar to 312,500,000 to 1. As you can see, done this way, the Five Rune Spread is absolutely personal and specific.

The term "Sacrifice," in the fourth position, is intended as a recognition that life offers you choices, options, that are often mutually exclusive. The concept of sacrifice has, over time, come to be associated primarily with pain and loss. As applied in the Five Rune Spread, however, the term refers to that which has to be peeled away, shed or discarded—as is called for in the Rune *Othila* ⧆ — in order for new wholeness to emerge. Originally a bonding of two Latin words, *sacrificium* and *facere*, one of the core meanings of sacrifice is "surrender to God."

A Sample Reading

Leila had created a successful business in partnership with her husband. The creative impulse of the idea, and the slogging hard work of getting the company on its feet, had been hers. The company was really "her baby." Now it was time to take the company public and the new investors wanted her participation but not her husband's. All her fears regarding loyalty, abandonment, the risk to her marriage and her husband's self-esteem were brought to the surface by this situation. So Leila decided to use the Five Rune Spread. She drew these Runes:

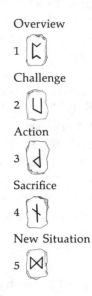

Overview

1

Challenge

2

Action

3

Sacrifice

4

New Situation

5

Drawing *Perth* ⟦ℾ⟧, the Rune of Initiation, as the *Overview* of the situation, immediately shifted her focus away from both her relationship with her husband and the business. "Nothing external matters here, except as it shows you its inner reflection"— these words were key for her. She read them over and over until she realized that this was another crossroad on the path of self-change.

In the *Challenge* position came *Uruz* ⟦ᚢ⟧, the Rune of Strength and Womanhood *Reversed*, indicating the need to respond consciously to "the demands of such a creative time." It was clear to her that growth at all levels—corporate as well as personal—was the correct decision.

The *Course of Action Called for* brought *Wunjo Reversed* ⟨◁⟩, which speaks of the process of birth being long and arduous, and about fears which arise for the safety of the child within. Again, the Runes were reminding Leila that she was undergoing a test.

The Rune of *Sacrifice* was *Nauthiz* ⟨↑⟩, the Rune of Constraint *Reversed*, the great teacher in the guise of pain and limitation. She was able to see more clearly that it was time to take a new kind of responsibility for what she had created, to own and honor it, and do what was good for the company.

Leila told me that she smiled with pleasure when she drew *Dagaz* ⟨⋈⟩, the Rune of Breakthrough, for the *New Situation Evolving*. This Rune offers the assurance that "because the timing is right, the outcome is assured, although not, from the present vantage point, predictable."

Several months after Leila's company had gone public, her husband started a new business which, thanks to his considerable talent, soon became a success.

THE RUNIC CROSS

This spread calls for selecting six Runes which are set out in the form of a Runic or Celtic Cross. The pattern is as follows:

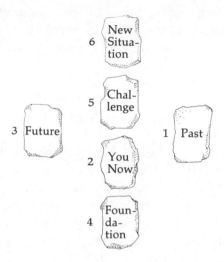

The first Rune represents the *Past*, that from which you are coming, what lies directly behind you. The second Rune represents *You Now*. The third, or *Future* Rune, stands for what lies ahead of you, what is coming into being in your life. The fourth Rune provides a look at the foundation of the matter under consideration, the unconscious elements and archetypal forces involved. The fifth, or *Challenge* Rune, suggests the nature of the obstacles in your path. The final Rune indicates the *New Situation* that will evolve as you successfully meet your challenge.

Since a considerable amount of information is contained in the Runic Cross, this spread often provides the incentive for deep thought and reflection. If, after laying out and considering these six Runes, you still lack sufficient clarity, draw a single Rune. This final Rune, the *Rune of Resolution*, will help you to recognize the essence of the situation.

THREE LIFETIMES SPREAD

This spread is for those who wish to experiment with the idea of reincarnation. It furnishes a three-level perspective on your passage, and is laid out in the form of the Rune of Fertility, *Inguz* ◊. The Runes represent (1) *Birth and Childhood Conditions*, (2) *Your Present*, (3) *Future in this Life*, (4) *Past Incarnation* and (5) *Future Incarnation*. The Runes are placed in the following manner:

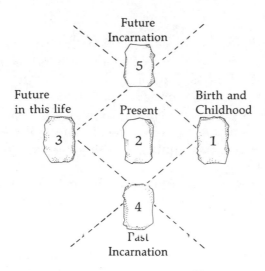

The Three Lifetimes Spread provides you with information concerning unresolved aspects of your past. Once these elements are recognized, you can seek to modify your present situation, thus affecting both your future in this life and your next soul cycle.

A Sample Reading

The first reading I undertook with the Three Lifetimes Spread was on my own account.

Birth and Childhood Conditions informs me that I came into this life to receive the gift of *Nauthiz* ⟨⟩, the Rune of Constraint and Pain. Now I must learn to work with the undeveloped aspects of myself, areas of stunted growth, weaknesses I project onto others. I am put on notice that I can expect setbacks all along my path until I understand the source of my suffering.

This Rune identifies my shadow, the disowned part of myself. It encourages me to pay attention to the judgments that I hold about others, to look within and discover what these judgments are telling me about myself and my own sense of inadequacy.

My *Present* is signified by *Jera* ⟨ᛃ⟩, the Rune of Harvest; it indicates a span of time leading to harvest during which I am called to exercise patience and cultivate my nature with care. In contemplating *Jera*, I am aware that preparing for the harvest requires me to pull up the weeds of anger and impatience—a daily task.

My *Future in this Life* is represented by *Sowelu* ⟨ᛋ⟩, the Rune of Wholeness and Life Force, the impulse toward self-realization and regeneration, the recognition of something long denied. *Something long denied*—that would be the need to have my self-esteem based not on material achievements, but on how I treat others and myself, on the way I conduct myself in the world.

Dagaz ⟨ᛞ⟩, the Rune of Transformation, stands in the *Past Incarnation* position. It indicates that a major transformation comes through addressing my own suffering and understanding its source. Everything in my life is telling me that I must dig down, confront and understand the source of my suffering in order to be made whole. How else will I learn compassion for others and for myself?

Finally, the *Future Incarnation* is represented by *Eihwaz* ⟨ᛇ⟩, the Rune of Defense and Avertive Powers. The only true defense is skillful means; that is to say, the realization of the qualities of patience, perseverance and resoluteness. These are the skillful means which will open the door to new life.

Over the years, since doing this reading, its accuracy has continued to sustain me. When I forget the wisdom of its counsel, I do so at my peril.

RUNE PLAY

This game is not about winning or losing. *Rune Play* focuses on whatever issue people want to examine, and play continues until such time as the issue seems adequately clarified to all players. If possible, each player should have a set of Runes, although one set will suffice. If only one bag of stones is used, however, the dynamics of the game are altered significantly.

Select three Runes and place them in front of you, glyph side down. The first player turns over a Rune and interprets it as it relates to the issue. Then, the next player turns over a Rune, gives an interpretation and has the option of relating it to the previous Rune. The third player turns over a Rune, offers an interpretation and has the option of commenting on the two previous Runes. When the round is completed, repeat the process for the second and third rounds. You may wish to play a final round in which the players, in turn, tell what new insights have come to them concerning the issue—and then have one person draw a final Rune as a commentary on those insights.

Rune Play can be enjoyed by a close-knit group of colleagues or associates working on a project. Say that you are developing a new product and the process is blocked. You may want to declare a Rune Play break. A variation on the Three Rune Spread might prove useful in such a situation: *You Now* (first round), *Your Part in the Blockage* (second round) and *Action Called for* (third round). The game swiftly takes on strategic and therapeutic overtones. Everyone will learn something, and there will be no lack of humor along the way.

In addition, this game can profitably be played by two people when a relationship issue calls for clarification. The number of Runes you choose is up to you. To keep friction at a minimum—if the situation is particularly sensitive—you may decide not to comment on one another's Runes until play is complete.

A Sample Game

A couple whose relationship was in trouble decided on a game of Rune Play. This is what followed: She played *Laguz Reversed* [J], the Rune of Water, Flow, That Which Conducts, interpreting it as counseling her husband to get in touch with the intuitive side of his nature in order to understand her better. He played *Raido* [R], the Rune of Journey, Communication, Union and Reunion, which he took as evidence of his willingness to keep on removing resistances and regulating excesses in his own life.

On the second round, she played *Hagalaz* [H], the Rune of Disruptive Natural Forces, Elemental Power, indicating an urge for freedom, a warning that she will, if necessary, sacrifice security and relationship in order to grow. He played *Uruz* [N], the Rune of Strength, Manhood, an indication that he, too, is going through a transition—reclaiming some part of himself, a part he has been living out through her.

As they continued to play, they became conscious of the fact that they were both in a period of accelerated self-change and needed to make an effort to hear each other more clearly.

A round of Rune Play can be most revealing although not, on every occasion, free of discomfort. But then growth rarely is.

THE CYCLE OF INITIATION

Thirteen of the twenty-five Runes focus directly on the mechanism of self-change. These Runes make up an energy framework within the body of the runic alphabet; an armature, so to speak, upholding and facilitating the process of self-change. You may find it useful to watch for the appearance of the Thirteen as you undergo your passage since, taken together, they comprise a *Cycle of Initiation*.

The Thirteen are:

(3)　*Ansuz* ᚠ, Signals, the Messenger Rune

(4)　*Othila* ᚷ, Separation, Retreat, Inheritance

(5)　*Uruz* ᚢ, Strength, Manhood/Womanhood

(6)　*Perth* ᚸ, Initiation, Something Hidden

(7)   *Nauthiz* ⟨↑⟩, Constraint, Necessity, Pain

(8)   *Inguz* ⟨◇⟩, Fertility, New Beginnings

(14) *Kano* ⟨⟨⟩, Opening, Fire

(16) *Berkana* ⟨B⟩, Growth, Rebirth

(17) *Ehwaz* ⟨M⟩, Movement, Progress

(19) *Hagalaz* ⟨H⟩, Disruption, Elemental Power

(20) *Raido* ⟨R⟩, Journey, Communication, Union, Reunion

(21) *Thurisaz* ⟨Þ⟩, Gateway, Place of Non-Action

(22) *Dagaz* ⟨M⟩, Breakthrough, Transformation

Whenever two or more of the Thirteen Cycle Runes are conjoint in a spread, the potential for growth and integration is considerably enhanced.

Technique

Isolate the thirteen Runes in their bag. Settle yourself quietly, aware that, rather than posing an issue for the Runes to comment upon, you are asking your Inner Knowing for direction, petitioning the Higher Self to advise you. Ask: *What in my life requires special attention? What aspect of my Nature, if cared for, modified, understood, nurtured, will carry me forward on the journey of the self toward the Self?*

Now draw a Rune to learn where you are in the

Cycle of Initiation. Does the Rune's estimate of your position accord with your own?

Next, draw a second Rune from all twenty-five stones in order to gain insight concerning how you can best complete this aspect of the Cycle.

This exercise can prove useful at times of transition or uncertainty by showing you where you are in the Cycle and helping you to prepare for the next step.

Sample Reading

Say that from the thirteen Cycle Runes you draw *Ansuz* ᚨ, Signals, the Messenger Rune. You are at the beginning of a new Cycle, *Ansuz* is telling you; this is the moment of new life unfolding. Now is the time to make conscious what is unconscious, particularly an awareness that self-nourishment is both possible and timely. You are asked to allow the Self to nourish the self, for it is only then that you will truly be in a position to nourish others.

The second Rune, drawn from all twenty-five, is *Thurisaz* ᚦ, the Gateway, which happens to be another of the Cycle Runes. *Thurisaz* urges you to contemplate your progress to date, the quality of your passage and the encounters that are taking place along your path. As you grow in clarity, new opportunities will be afforded you.

From the self to the Self the word goes out; from the Self to the Divine. By heeding the call of the Cycle of Initiation, you are indeed opening yourself to the message of the Divine in your life.

KEEPING A RUNE JOURNAL

As you establish your practice of working with the Runes, you may find it helpful to keep track of the guidance you receive. Record your issue, the particular stones cast, and a brief interpretation in your journal.* Note the time, date and the prevailing conditions in your life at the moment. Many people have experienced one particular Rune appearing in their readings over and over again, only to be replaced in time by another Rune which similarly reoccurs. It is as if the Oracle is saying, "This is where you are blocked. This is where work needs to be done." Keeping a journal allows you to recognize your patterns as you progress in the art of self-change.

RULE OF RIGHT ACTION

A technique that Dr. Allan W. Anderson suggested to students of the *I Ching* is equally valid for those who work with the Runes. He called it *The Rule of Right Action*. Each morning consult the Oracle to determine your Rule of Right Action for the day. Draw one Rune, record it in your journal, and let it serve as your guidance for that day. Sometimes, when your day has been particularly trying or exhilarating, you may wish to consult the

*Rune Play, A Seasonal Record Book with Twelve New Techniques for Rune Casting, by Ralph Blum, was published by St. Martin's Press in 1985.

Oracle again in the evening for an evaluation of how you've conducted yourself. If the idea of asking daily seems excessive, do so on a weekly basis. Consult the Runes on Monday for the week's Rule of Right Action, then draw another Rune on Sunday night for the evaluation.

Recording these readings in your Rune Journal will help you to become more familiar with the Runes and their symbolism and will, over time, enable you to judge for yourself the relevance and accuracy of the Oracle as an appropriate guide to self-change.

* * *

Ancient as they are, the Viking Runes remain an open-ended system. In time, you will no doubt discover new and creative ways to use them. Enjoy your Runes, play with them, let them speak to you. We at the RuneWorks would appreciate hearing from you about your own experiences with the Oracle.

A SIMPLE PRAYER

Lord, make me an instrument of your peace.
Where there is hatred, let me sow love.
Where there is injury, let me sow pardon.
Where there is doubt, let me sow faith.
Where there is despair, let me sow hope.
Where there is sadness, let me sow joy.
O Divine Master, grant that
I may not so much seek
To be consoled as to console,
To be understood as to understand,
To be loved as to love.
For it is in giving that we receive.
It is in pardoning that we are pardoned.
It is in dying that we are born to eternal life.

—St. Francis of Assisi

Darbyshire bone piece,
English, eighth century

5

RUNECRAFT: THREE CEREMONIAL SPREADS

God loves the world through us.

—Mother Teresa

In our contemporary world of instant everything, these three exercises call us to remember the cyclical nature of life and personal growth. Whether it takes the form of cleansing, setting things right in a relationship or the completion of one of life's cycles, taking the time to acknowledge and make conscious what you are about to do will invariably enrich your experience.

The exercises which follow are intended to facilitate the reintroduction of ritual—and hence the sacred—into our daily lives.

WATER RUNES

This exercise is linked to the Rune *Laguz* ⟨↑⟩, whose attributes are "water, fluidity, the ebb and flow of emotions, of vocations and relationships." It is a

68

cleansing, healing ritual that can be performed whenever your body comes in contact with water.

Before you dip your hands into water, take a shower, jump into a pool, a pond, or the ocean, pause a moment to think or speak these words:

> *I cleanse myself of all selfishness,*
> *Resentment,*
> *Critical feelings for my fellow being,*
> *Self-condemnation,*
> *And misinterpretation of my life experiences.*

Observe what comes to mind as you repeat this *Prayer of Intention* aloud or in silence. Say the words with love and gentleness, for you are not making yourself wrong. Rather, you are embodying in words a yearning for more clarity, more light in your life.

Then again, you may prefer to reframe the negative attributes of selfishness, resentment, and self-condemnation into their *light opposites*, repeating the prayer in the following form:

> *I bathe myself in generosity,*
> *Appreciation,*
> *Praise and gratitude for my fellow beings,*
> *Self-acceptance,*
> *And enlightened understanding of my life*
>   *experiences.*

Select a Rune on the issue of self-condemnation or self-acceptance on one day. On another day you might draw a Rune relating to selfishness or generosity. You may wish to draw a Rune concerning a particular life experience that has become fixed in memory as distasteful, shameful or embarrassing, asking for new light by which to grow in understanding of the truth and appropriateness of that experience.

The occasions for using the *Water Runes* are limitless. There is no activity that is less sacred than any other. Washing the dishes, the dog or the pickup will do nicely, as will bathing the baby, watering the lawn, swimming in the Black Sea or standing in the London or Seattle rain.

You may wish to write out this Prayer of Intention and tape it to the shower wall, the splashboard over your sink, the water cooler. When the words run and dissolve, write them out and stick them up again. Let the Water Runes Ceremony flow with your life.

RUNES OF RECTIFICATION

rectify 1. to put or set right; correct; amend; 2. to adjust, as in movement or balance . . .

—*Webster's New World Dictionary*

This is a technique for those times when problems arise between co-workers, friends, lovers and others who collaborate across boundaries of understanding and temperament.

When something occurs that causes dissension or

blockage between you, come together with the intention of bringing light to the situation. Here the procedure is reversed, in that the Rune casting comes at the *end* of the process. The core of this ritual consists of asking and answering five questions:

(1) What happened?
(2) How do you feel about what happened?
(3) How would you do it differently next time?
(4) What results would you like to see?
(5) What insight have you gained from
    this experience?

Close the door and unplug the telephone. Be sure to allow enough time a) for all participants to answer each question, b) for discussion and, c) for the drawing of Runes to further clarify the issue.

One person may elect to take notes while the others speak. Each question should be addressed by all of the participants before proceeding to the next question. Cross-talk or responding to someone while they are speaking is to be discouraged. Statements of *how you feel* (hurt, angry, self-conscious, afraid) rather than accusatory statements of "what you did to me" or "what you did wrong" will help to keep the discussion from dissolving into self-justification or acrimony. During this process, agree to suspend judgment for the sake of better understanding.

After everyone has had the opportunity to express their feelings, encourage any of the participants who still require clarification on a particular issue to pick a Rune. One of you might be disturbed or confused about emotions you expressed in answer to question #2, *How do you feel about what happened?* Or perhaps there is some disagreement about what actually took place. If so, further insight can be provided by selecting a Rune to comment on question #1, *What happened?* Continue picking Runes to clarify your questions until resolution and harmony are reached. You may be surprised at how quickly this occurs.

When all is said and done, one of you may wish to draw a final Rune to comment on the essence of the matter in the light of the process of rectification.

RUNES OF COMFORT FOR THE BEREAVED

If you have unfinished business with someone who has died, simply take a moment to visualize the person you want to remember. Use a favorite photograph if you have one. Then make a list of the matters you would have liked to discuss, the things you wish you had shared but didn't. Draw a Rune on each issue and meditate on the response. Letters received from people who have worked with the Runes in this way indicate that the results are invariably helpful and heartening.

A young man whose mother had recently been killed in an automobile accident wanted to know what she would have advised him before she died. He drew *Teiwaz* ↑, the Warrior Rune. "Be a Spiritual

Warrior," he wrote. "That's exactly what she would have said!"

"When my grief was choking me," wrote a Florida woman about the death of her twin sister, "I picked a Rune on the issue *What would Clara be saying to me now?* and received *Inguz* ⟨◊⟩, Fertility and New Beginnings. I had to laugh. I had just kept my promise to spread her ashes on the roses!"

This process is not to be confused with séances or night letters from beyond the veil. Perhaps what the Runes do here is access your deep knowing about the person, knowing which is lodged in your own sub-conscious. When we hear the voice of truth, we recognize it.

The prayer that follows is the result of a meditation on one such Rune casting when *Dagaz* ⟨⋈⟩, the Rune of Breakthrough and Transformation, was drawn.

Detail from the Franks' Casket,
whale bone, eighth century

RUNES OF COMFORT
FOR THE BEREAVED

I am the Life and the Light and the Way.
The earth is my garden.
Each of the souls I plant as seeds
Germinates and flowers in its season
And in each I am fulfilled.
There is no cause for grief
When a blossom fades
But only rejoicing for the beauty it held
And praise that my will is done
And my plan served.
I am one with all creatures
And none is ever lost
But only restored to me
Having never left me at all.
For what is Eternal
Cannot be separated from its Source.
I am with you all,
And each of you is a channel for my Light.
Feel my Love
Enfold you now and evermore.

6

A DESTINY
PROFILE

The task is to define oneself, for oneself, in a manner that enables a relationship to oneself. In so doing, one becomes who one truly is.

—Dr. Allan W. Anderson

What is within surrounds us.

—Rainer Maria Rilke

In undertaking the work of self-change, we are asked to examine the foundations of our lives. We hear it said in many camps, by spiritual teachers of all persuasions, that we are to "discover the teacher within." What we need now are some useful techniques for listening to ourselves.

One such technique was devised by Dr. Allan W. Anderson for use with the *I Ching*, the Chinese *Book of Changes*. He called it *A Destiny Profile*. The Profile, which consists of six questions, comprises a grid within which a human life can be framed. The questions are:

(1) *What is my Nature?*
(2) *Why was I Born?*
(3) *What is my Vocation?*
(4) *What is my Destiny?*
(5) *What is my Cross?*
(6) *What is my Unified Self?*

The Destiny Profile adapts itself well to use with the Viking Runes. However, there is a seriousness about this spread that sets it apart from other runic exercises. According to Dr. Anderson, the six questions that make up the Profile shall be asked *only once* in the course of one's lifetime. This restriction may at first seem daunting, especially in our "try, try again" culture. We don't like limitation. And yet, the very gift of the Destiny Profile is that it teaches us to understand *the creative essence of limitation*.

When I asked, "What are we to be made conscious of through the Destiny Profile?" the Oracle replied with *Laguz Reversed* ⟨↑⟩, the Rune of Flow, Water: *A warning against overreach, excessive striving, a counsel against trying to exceed your own strength or operate beyond the power you have funded to date in your life.* According to the Oracle, then, The Destiny Profile does indeed focus on the nature of limitation.

You may wish to defer drawing the Runes for the Destiny Profile until you have considered the idea for a while. Long thoughts about the way you have lived your life until now may be appropriate before you proceed. When you are ready to begin, perhaps you will want to ask the first question, receive the Oracle's commentary, then consider that commentary for a time before proceeding to the next question. Or you may elect to ask all six questions at a single sitting, then study them one at a time over an extended period.

After drawing a Rune for the first question, record it, then replace the Rune in the bag. *Each question must be posed with a complete set of Runes.* When recording the Runes that you draw, place them in a vertical line with the first Rune at the top, and then write down your thoughts about the Oracle's response. You may wish to review your Destiny Profile from time to time, adding new insights as they occur to you.

Here, then, is a commentary on the six questions that comprise the Destiny Profile, each followed by a sample reading.

(1) WHAT IS MY NATURE?

In asking the question "What is my Nature?" you are concerning yourself with the material cause of your being, the possibilities you were born with. For while your Nature is a constellation of possibilities, it is also surrounded and circumscribed by numerous impossibilities.

Begin by examining your limitations: You come

from a certain background, you have lived your life in a particular way, you have a heart condition, you can't have children—whatever the case may be. As your limitations become clearer to you, you will begin to see that various notions you hold about yourself are not supported by the reality of your life. And yet, just as your Nature is *limited* by what you cannot do or be, it is also *specified* by what you can. Through this process of limiting and specifying, your view of yourself will become clearer and more simple. As you simplify, you fund the power to work with your Nature, with the substance out of which your Destiny is to be realized.

A Sample Reading

Ehwaz ⋈, The Rune of Movement, Progress, *Reversed*. This Rune is concerned with movement that appears to block. It speaks to the difficulty you have in recognizing what is timely to your Nature and what is not. First, work on yourself to strengthen your connection with the Divine; when that connection is strong enough, what needs to be accomplished will become apparent to you. The feeling that you are missing out will be replaced by the desire to avoid action until it is timely. However, if you insist on pushing ahead unstrengthened, your nature will turn against everything you do that is premature, for Destiny cannot be humbugged or manipulated. There is an old saying that "What is for you will not pass by you." Or, as *Ehwaz* expresses it, "As I cultivate my own nature, all else follows."

(2) WHY WAS I BORN?

The meaning of the question is this: What is the lack or privation with which I have come into the world, whose satisfaction will empower my continuing growth in keeping with the Will of the Divine? In other words, *What is Heaven's mandate for me?* In addressing this question, you are preparing to discover what is missing from your makeup that you are here to acquire—patience, courage in the face of adversity, the growth of a will, or any other underdeveloped aspect of your self—the acquiring of which will enable you to navigate your ideal passage through this life.

A Sample Reading

Sowelu ⟨ϟ⟩, the Rune of Wholeness, stands for that which your Nature requires. One mark of the Spiritual Warrior is impeccability. *Living impeccably means to strive at all times to do what is appropriate.* To achieve this end, you are required to "face and vanquish your refusal to let right action flow through you."

The task of a Spiritual Warrior is to seek after Wholeness, to bring together those aspects of the self that require unification. This Rune also focuses on the ability to retreat while you still have strength. In timely retreat, allow the light to enter any part of your being which has been kept in darkness. That darkness—the result of privation and denial—is the dungeon of the divided self. Timely right action will lead you to self-acceptance, self-healing and, eventually, to Wholeness.

(3) WHAT IS MY VOCATION?

Vocation, as used here, does not mean what you do for a living. Drawing a Rune for Vocation will tell you how you are called to go through this life and what principles you must embody in your passage. If you conduct yourself correctly according to Vocation, you will satisfy the privation or lack described in the answer to the question *"Why was I Born?"* By learning to relate correctly to severe privation, you grow in the Spirit. That is why St. Paul says in Romans 4: "We rejoice in tribulations," since tribulations provide the occasions to meet privation courageously. In the process, you will grow in self-awareness and strengthen your will. The principal goal of Vocation is to come to one's Self.

A Sample Reading

Ehwaz $\lceil M \rceil$, Movement, Progress, specifies that your Vocation calls for movement in the sense of improving or bettering any situation. Note that this same Rune was drawn Reversed in answer to the question *"What is my Nature?"* Drawing *Ehwaz* twice in the Profile emphasizes the idea of timely movement as crucial to the exercising of right action.

Simply expressed, the principle is this: no acting

needy, no lusting after outcomes. Learn how to wait. Learn how to ask. Learn how to go solitarily through the world. Then your Vocation ⟨M⟩, will agree with your Nature ⟨W⟩, and all movement will be in accord with the Will of Heaven.

There is a process, practiced by my friend the Reverend Harry Haines, that seems relevant to the work required of us as regards Vocation. Whenever he is called upon to deal with an issue where clarity is lacking, before acting, he does four things: "First I consider my own needs. Then I consider the needs of others. Next, I consult a wiser Christian. And finally, I wait for the peace that passes understanding. Only then will I act."

(4) WHAT IS MY DESTINY?

Destiny, as used here, means *your ideal passage through this life, your ideal possibility*. There is no such thing as a bad Destiny, for your Destiny is the Divine's desire for your Highest Good. An energy exists that ceaselessly moves us to change for good rather than ill, and that energy is the outworking of Divine Will in our lives. Your Destiny is your spiritual destination.

At the same time, Destiny means confinement, for your Destiny is realized as the direct result of life's limitations. According to *Ehwaz*, there are no missed opportunities: You have simply to recognize that not all possibilities are open to you, that not all opportunities are appropriate. If your limitations define what you may not do in the world, they also challenge you to accept yourself and get on with what is yours to achieve.

A Sample Reading

In drawing *Perth* ⟦⟧, the Rune of Initiation, *Reversed*, you are reminded that "Nothing external matters here, except as it shows you its inner reflection." *Perth* has associations with the Phoenix, "the mystical bird that consumes itself in the fire and then rises from its own ashes." Again and again, the Oracle is saying, you will go through the flames. Treat each obstruction in your path as a challenge specific to the initiation you are presently undergoing. By living your life as Initiation and responding well to the Will of Heaven, you cannot fail to satisfy the requirements of your Destiny.

(5) WHAT IS MY CROSS?

The Cross stands for a condition that lasts a lifetime; it is your ordeal from birth to death. The answer to this question reveals the pattern of adversity you must undergo in order to increase in self-awareness and self-rule. Take up your Cross voluntarily. For in so doing you are declaring your willingness to undergo the pattern of adversity ordained for you by

Divine Will. As you grow in awareness, you will come to recognize that certain features of adversity are yours to work with throughout your life. Many opportunities will be afforded you to meet the challenges represented by your Cross.

The Cross is the condition for wisdom. Christ on the Tree. Odin on the Tree. Each of us on the Tree. The Cross stands for that without which there can be no getting of wisdom.

A Sample Reading

Eihwaz ⟨ᛇ⟩, Defense, Avertive Powers. "As we are tested we fund the power to avert blockage and defeat," this Rune is saying. Learn to regard delays and blockages as potentially beneficial and you will come to realize that, through inconvenience and discomfort, growth is promoted.

There is a tendency in your Nature to surpass the limits proper to that Nature. This tendency—to push beyond where good can be achieved—calls for a Cross, a pattern of adversity; it calls for your being thwarted each time your actions are inappropriate. And yet, ultimately, all that is asked of you is to go through the world well.

(6) WHAT IS MY UNIFIED SELF?

In seeking the image of your Unified Self, ask for the qualities that will emerge in your life when your intellect and will begin to work in harmony with your physical being and your heart. To act uncontrivedly and in a timely manner are signs that you are in accord with your Unified Self. Seek to discover the Teacher Within, for then you have a reliable source for understanding the component forces with which you must work in order to become your Unified Self.

A Sample Reading

Uruz ⋂, Strength, Manhood, Womanhood. The image of the Unified Self will emerge as the old bonds are severed, when that which has outgrown its form has died, releasing its energy in a new birth, a new form. The Rune of terminations and new beginnings, *Uruz* exemplifies a willingness on your part to embrace change and to recognize and remember that, in the life of the Spirit, you are always at the beginning.

In ancient times, *Uruz* was symbolized by the aurochs, the wild ox, a difficult animal to domesticate. Drawing this Rune in response to the question *"What is my Unified Self?"* indicates that to achieve self-unification, you must undertake to gentle the wild creature within. This can only be accomplished by becoming one with it through your compassionate understanding of its nature and needs. Develop your will by setting your intention and by visualizing the form your Unified Self will take. With time, that form will expand; as you embrace the image of the expanded form, it will continue to evolve and self-understanding will increase.

* * *

The Destiny Profile is a tool to be used as you persevere in the finest art of all, the art of self-change. Remember: Self-change is never coerced; we are always free to resist. And if there is one thing to bear in mind until the truth of its words eases the heart troubled by apparent failure and loss, it is this: *The new life is always greater than the old.*

Once the elements of your Destiny Profile have been identified, you will begin to see how they fit together. Through focusing on the correlation between "What is my Vocation?" (the occasion for acquiring strength) and "Why was I Born?" (the privation with which you came into the world), you can begin to relate correctly to undeveloped and disowned aspects of your self. As your knowledge of your self increases, so will self-acceptance, and you will experience the meaning and joy of living your life in true present time. It is through letting go of your attachments to the past and your expectations for the future that you will experience a true present, which is the only time in which self-change can be realized.

Finally, as you change and grow, your understanding of the six readings in your Destiny Profile will also change and grow—grow, perhaps, to include an appreciation that asking the questions only once is enough.

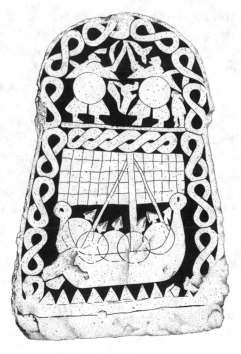

Picture stone at När Smiss,
Gotland, Sweden

A WARRIOR'S CREED

I have no parents—*I make the heavens and earth my parents.*

I have no home—*I make awareness my home.*

I have no life or death—*I make the tides of breathing my life and death.*

I have no divine power—*I make honesty my divine power.*

I have no means—*I make understanding my means.*

I have no magic secrets—*I make character my magic secret.*

I have no body—*I make endurance my body.*

I have no eyes—*I make the flash of lightning my eyes.*

I have no ears—*I make sensibility my ears.*

I have no limbs—*I make promptness my limbs.*

I have no strategy—*I make "unshadowed by thought" my strategy.*

I have no designs—*I make "seizing opportunity by the forelock" my design.*

I have no miracles—*I make right-action my miracles.*

I have no principles—*I make adaptability to all circumstances my principles.*

I have no tactics—*I make emptiness and fullness my tactics.*

I have no talents—*I make ready wit my talent.*

I have no friends—*I make my mind my friend.*

I have no enemy—*I make carelessness my enemy.*

I have no armor—*I make benevolence and righteousness my armor.*

I have no castle—*I make immovable-mind my castle.*

I have no sword—*I make absence of self my sword.*

—Anonymous Samurai, fourteenth century

LEGACY OF THE RUNES

*The seed of God is in us. . . . Pear seeds grow into pear trees,
hazel seeds into hazel trees, and God seeds into God.*

—Meister Eckhart

The final part of this book is the only part you really need—that and your set of Rune stones. In approaching an ancient mystery a surrender is required. As the Sufi poet Rumi wrote: "Let the beauty we love be what we do/There are hundreds of ways to kneel and kiss the ground."

Imagine a vast and misty field containing a Stonehenge that did not survive. It lies within view of a glacier, this field, high above the mouth of a wild fjord. Out of the mist emerges a circle of massive weathered stones brushed with yellow lichen. Above the rustle of feather grass, the deeply carved glyphs in the center of each stone seem to pulse and vibrate. In the middle of the circle, touched by the sun's first rays, stands a blank and solitary stone: *Both pregnant and empty, arbiter of all that is coming to be and passing away . . .*

These stones are the markers left by Spiritual

Warriors, the servants of civilization. Hundreds of years have passed. The voices that once whispered to others now whisper to us. And to hear them? All that is required is for you to honor your own nature and know the stillness within. To that end when consulting the Runes, a single question, a simple prayer, will always suffice: *Show me what I need to know for my life now.*

A Rune stone by the famous carver,
Balle Väfrukyrka, Uppland, Sweden

8

RUNE
INTERPRETATIONS

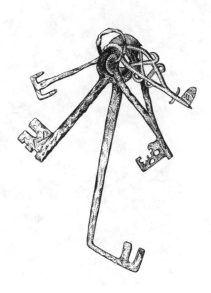

The Self

The starting point is the self. Its essence is water. Only clarity, willingness to change, is effective now. A correct relationship to your self is primary, for from it flow all possible right relationships with others and with the Divine.

Remain modest—that is the Oracle's counsel. Regardless of how great may be your merit, be yielding, devoted and moderate, for then you have a true direction for your life.

Be in the world but not of it. And yet do not be closed, narrow, or judging; rather, remain receptive to impulses flowing from the Divine within and without. *Strive to live the ordinary life in a nonordinary way.* Remember at all times what is coming to be and passing away, and focus on that which abides. Nothing less is called for from you now.

This is a time of major growth and rectification and, as a rule, rectification must come before progress. The field is tilled before the seed is planted, the garden is weeded before the flower blooms, and the self must know stillness before it can discover its true song.

Now is not a time to seek credit for accomplishments or to focus on results. Instead, be content to do your task for the task's sake. Herein lies the secret of experiencing a *true present*.

If you take the Rune of the Self and cut it down the middle, you will see the Rune for Joy with its mirror image. There is here a subtle caution against carelessness. The Self is required to balance the self.

Nothing in excess was the second phrase written over the gateway to the temple at Delphi. The first counsel was *Know thyself*.

Reversed: If you feel blocked, *Mannaz* urges you to begin by being clear with yourself. Do not turn to others now, but look inside, in silence, for the enemy of your progress. No matter what area of your life is in disarray, stop and consider: You will recognize the outer enemy as but a reflection of what you have not, until now, been able or willing to recognize as coming from within.

Above all do not give yourself airs. Breaking the momentum of past habits is the challenge here: In the life of the Spirit, you are always at the beginning.

Partnership
A Gift

Drawing this Rune is an indication that partnership in some form is at hand. In love relationships, in business matters, in partnering of every kind, you are put on notice not to collapse yourself into that union. For true partnership is achieved only by separate and whole beings who retain their separateness even as they unite. Remember to let the winds of Heaven dance between you.

At the same time, there is another aspect of partnership that you are being called to consider. For the path of partnership can lead you to the realization of a still greater union—union with the Higher Self, union with the Divine. The ultimate gift of this Rune is the realization of the Divine in all things: God always enters into equal partnerships.

Gebo, the Rune of Partnership, has no Reverse, for it signifies the gift of freedom from which flow all other gifts.

3

Ansuz

Signals
Messenger Rune
The God Loki

The keynote here is receiving: messages, signals, gifts. Even a timely warning may be seen as a gift. The message may be that of a new life unfolding. New lives begin with new connections, surprising linkages that direct you onto new pathways. Take care now to be especially aware during meetings, visits, chance encounters, particularly with persons wiser than yourself. When the Messenger Rune brings sacred knowledge, you are truly blessed.

Loki is the ancient trickster from the pantheon of the Norse gods. He is the *heyeohkah* of the Native Americans, a mocking shadow of the creator god, as well as the bringer of benefits to humankind. He is a reminder that even scoundrels and arch-thieves can be the bearers of wisdom. When you draw this Rune, expect the unexpected: The message is always a call, a call to new life.

Ansuz is the first of the thirteen Runes that make up the Cycle of Initiation—Runes that focus directly upon the mechanism of self-change—and as such, addresses our need to integrate unconscious motive with conscious intent.

Drawing *Ansuz* tells you that connection with the Divine is at hand. It is a signal to explore the depths, the foundations of life, and to experience the inexhaustible wellspring of the Divine in your nature.

At the same time, you are reminded that you must first draw from the well to nourish and give to yourself. Then there will be more than enough to nourish others. A new sense of family solidarity invests this Rune.

Reversed: You may be concerned over what appears to be failed communication, lack of clarity or awareness either in your past history or in a present situation. You may feel inhibited from accepting what is offered. A sense of futility, of wasted motion, may overwhelm you. Remember, however, that what is happening is timely to your process. If the well is clogged, this is the moment for cleaning out the old. Reversed, *Ansuz* is saying: *Consider the uses of adversity.*

4

Othila

Separation

Retreat

Inheritance

This is a time of separating paths. Old skins must be shed, outmoded relationships discarded. When you receive this Rune, a peeling away is called for. Part of the Cycle of Initiation, *Othila* is a Rune of radical severance.

The appropriate action here is submission and, quite possibly, retreat—knowing how and when to retreat and possessing the firmness of will to carry it out.

Real property is associated with *Othila*, for it is the Rune of acquisition and benefits. However, the benefits you receive—the Inheritance—may be derived from something you must give up. This can be particularly demanding when what you are called upon to abandon is some aspect of your behavior, a part of your cultural Inheritance. For then you must look closely at what, until now, you have proudly claimed as your birthright. Whether it is your attachment to your position in society, to the work you do, or even to your beliefs about your own nature, the separation called for will free you to become more truly who you are.

X **Reversed**: This is not a time to be bound by old conditioning, old authority. Consider not only what will benefit you but what will benefit others, and act according to the light you possess now in your life. Because you may be called upon to undertake a radical departure from old ways, total honesty is required. Otherwise, through negligence or refusal to see clearly, you may cause pain to others and damage to yourself.

Adaptability and skillful means are the methods to cultivate at this time. And still you must wait for the universe to act. Receiving this Rune, remember: *We do without doing and everything gets done.*

5
Uruz

Strength
Manhood, Womanhood
The Wild Ox

The Rune of terminations and new beginnings, drawing *Uruz* indicates that the life you have been living has outgrown its form. That form must die so that new energy can be released in a new form. This is a Rune of passage and, as such, part of the Cycle of Initiation.

Positive growth and change, however, may involve a descent into darkness as part of the cycle of perpetual renewal. As in nature, this progression consists of five aspects: death, decay, fertilization, gestation, rebirth. Events occurring now may well prompt you to undergo a death within yourself. Since self-change is never coerced—we are always free to resist—remain mindful that the new life is always greater than the old.

Prepare, then, for opportunity disguised as loss. It could involve the loss of someone or something to which you have an intense emotional bond, and through which you are living a part of your life, a part that must now be retrieved so you can live it out for yourself. In some way, that bond is being severed, a relationship radically changed, a way of life coming to an end. Seek among the ashes and discover a new perspective and new strength.

The ancient symbol for *Uruz* was the aurochs, a wild ox. When the wild ox was domesticated—an immensely difficult task—it could transport heavy loads. Learn to adapt yourself to the demands of such a creative time. Firm principles attach to this Rune. At the same time humility is called for, since in order to rule you must learn how to serve. *Uruz* puts you on notice that your soul and the universe support the new growth.

Reversed: Without ears to hear and eyes to see, you may fail to take advantage of the moment. The result could well be an opportunity missed or the weakening of your position. It may seem that your own strength is being used against you.

For some, *Uruz Reversed* will serve to alert, offering clues in the form of minor failures and disappointments. For others, those more deeply unconscious or unaware, it may provide a hard jolt. Reversed, this Rune calls for serious thought about the quality of your relationship to your Self.

But take heart. Consider the constant cycling of

death and rebirth, the endless going and return. Everything we experience has a beginning, a middle and an end, and is followed by a new beginning. Therefore do not draw back from the passage into darkness: When in deep water, become a diver.

Initiation

Something Hidden

A Secret Matter

A hieratic or mystery Rune pointing to that which is beyond our frail manipulative powers. *Perth* is on the side of Heaven, the Unknowable, and has associations with the phoenix, that mystical bird which consumes itself in the fire and then rises from its own ashes. Its ways are secret and hidden.

Powerful forces of change are at work here. Yet what is achieved is not easily or readily shared. After all, becoming whole—the means of it—is a profound secret.

On the side of the earthly or mundane, there may well be surprises, gains or rewards that you did not anticipate. On the side of human nature, this Rune is symbolized by the flight of the eagle. Soaring flight, free from entanglement, lifting yourself above the endless ebb and flow of ordinary life to acquire broader vision—all this is indicated here.

Another of the Cycle Runes, *Perth* stands at the heart of Initiation. *Nothing external matters here, except as it shows you its inner reflection.* This Rune is concerned with the deepest stratum of our being, the bedrock on which our destiny is founded. For some, *Perth* means experiencing a death. If need be, let go of everything, no exceptions, no exclusions. Nothing less than renewal of the Spirit is at stake.

Reversed: A counsel against expecting too much, or expecting in the ordinary way, for the old way has come to an end: You simply cannot repeat the old and not suffer. Call in your scattered energies, concentrate on your own life at this moment, your own requirements for growth. *Perth* counsels you neither to focus on outcomes nor to bind yourself with the memory of past achievements. In doing so, you rob yourself of a *true present,* the only time in which self-change can be realized.

You may feel overwhelmed with exhaustion from meeting obstruction upon obstruction in your passage. Yet always you have a choice: You can see this apparent negativity as bad luck, or you can recognize it as an obstacle course, a challenge specific to the Initiation you are presently undergoing. Then each setback, each humiliation, becomes a test of character. When your inner being is shifting and reforming on a deep level, patience, constancy and perseverance are called for. So stay centered, see the humor, and keep your faith firm.

Constraint

Necessity

Pain

7
Nauthiz

The necessity of learning to deal with severe constraint is the lesson of *Nauthiz*. This Rune represents the obstacles we create for ourselves as well as those we encounter in the world around us. Both can be equally difficult to handle.

The role of *Nauthiz* is to identify our shadow, our dark or repressed side, places where growth has been stunted, resulting in weaknesses that are often projected onto others. *Don't take this world personally*, this Rune is saying: Work with the shadow, examine what it is in your nature that attracts hardship or misfortune to your life. When at last you can look upon the Rune of Constraint with a smile, you will recognize the troubles, denials and setbacks of life as your teachers, guides and allies.

The need for restraint is unquestionable here. Drawing this Rune indicates that there may well be holdups and reasons to reconsider your plans carefully. Clearly, there is work to be done on yourself. So take it on with good humor and show perseverance.

This is a time to pay off old debts, to restore, if not harmony, at least balance. So mend, restore, redress: When fisherman can't go to sea they repair nets. Let the constraints of the time serve you in righting your relationship to your Self. Be mindful that rectification must come before progress. And as always, consider the uses of adversity.

Reversed: As part of the Cycle of Initiation, *Nauthiz* is the great teacher disguised as the bringer of pain and limitation. It has been said that only at the moment of greatest darkness do we become aware of the light within and come to recognize the true creative power of the self.

When something within you is disowned, that which is disowned wreaks havoc. A cleansing is required here; in undertaking it, you fund a will and strengthen character. Begin with what is most difficult and proceed to that which is easy. Or, conversely, begin with what is easy and proceed to that which is most difficult. Either way, remember that "suffering," in its original sense, merely meant "undergoing." Thus you are required to undergo the dark side of your passage and bring it into the light. Controlling your anger, restraining your impulses, keeping your faith firm—all this is at issue here. Modesty and good temper are essential at such a challenging time.

Fertility
New Beginnings
Ing, the Hero God

This Rune is akin to the moon, the intuitive part
of our nature, with its urge toward harmonizing and
adjusting in the sphere of personal relationships.
Inguz embodies the need to share, the yearning to be
desired, a search after similarities.

The completion of beginnings is what *Inguz* requires.
Drawing this Rune may mark a time of joyful deliverance, of new life, a new path. A Rune of great power,
receiving it means that you now have the strength to
achieve completion, resolution, from which comes a
new beginning. Above all, completion is crucial here.
It may be timely that you complete some project now;
if so, make that your first priority. Perhaps a difficult
state of mind can be clarified or resolved. The appearance of this Rune indicates that you must fertilize the
ground for your own deliverance.

All things change and we cannot live perma-
nently amid obstructions. *Inguz* signals your emer-
gence from a closed, chrysalis state. As you resolve

and clear away the old, you will experience a release from tension and uncertainty.

You may be required to free yourself from a rut, habit or relationship; from some deep cultural or behavioral pattern, some activity that was quite proper to the self you are leaving behind. The time of birth is always a critical one. Movement can involve danger, and yet movement that is timely leads out of danger. The time has come to enter the delivery room.

Another of the Cycle Runes, *Inguz* counsels preparation. Being centered and grounded, freeing yourself from all unwanted influences and seeing the humor, you are indeed prepared to open to the Will of Heaven and await your deliverance with calm certainty.

Defense
Avertive Powers
Yew Tree

As we are tested we fund the power to avert blockage and defeat. At the same time, we develop in ourselves an aversion to the conduct that creates stress in our lives.

If there appears to be an obstacle in your path, consider that even a delay may prove beneficial. Do not be overly eager to press forward, for this is not a time or situation in which you can make your influence felt. Patience is the counsel *Eihwaz* offers: nothing hectic, no acting needy, or lusting after a desired outcome. This Rune speaks to the difficulties that can arise at the beginning of a new life. Often it announces a time of waiting—for a spring to fill up with water, for fruit to ripen on the bough.

Perseverance and foresight are called for here. *The ability to foresee consequences before you act is a mark of the profound person.* Avert anticipated difficulties through right action, this Rune is saying. And yet even more than we are *doers*, we are *deciders*. Once the decision is clear, the doing becomes effortless, for then the universe supports and empowers our action.

Receiving *Eihwaz*, you are put on notice that, through inconvenience and discomfort, growth is promoted. This may well be a trying time; certainly it is a meaningful one. So set your house in order, tend to business, be clear, and wait on the Will of Heaven.

Algiz

Protection
Sedge or Rushes
The Elk

Control of the emotions is at issue here. During times of transition, shifts in life course and accelerated self-change, it is important not to collapse yourself into your emotions, the highs as well as the lows. New opportunities and challenges are typical of this Rune. And with them may come trespasses and unwanted influences.

Algiz serves as a mirror for the Spiritual Warrior, the one whose battle is always with the self. The Warrior's protection is like the curved horns of the elk, or the warning rustle of the sedge grass, for both serve to keep open space around you.

Remain mindful that timely right action and correct conduct are your only true protection. If you find yourself feeling pain, observe the pain, stay with it. Do not try to pull down the veil and escape from life by denying what is happening. You *will* progress; knowing that is your protection.

Reversed: Be thoughtful about your health and do not add to the burdens others are carrying. Look carefully at the associations you form at this time. If you see fit to become involved with people who are using you, remain conscious of that fact and take responsibility for your own position; then you can only benefit. And yet, regardless of whether your enterprise prospers or suffers, do not be overly concerned. You may not win, but you will never lose, for you can always learn from what takes place.

Temperance and courtesy are the sinews of this Rune's protective powers.

Possessions
Nourishment
Cattle

Fehu is a Rune of fulfillment: ambition satisfied, love shared, rewards received. It promises nourishment from the most worldly to the sacred and the Divine. For if the ancient principle "As above so below" holds true, then we are also here to nourish God.

This Rune calls for a deep probing of the meaning of profit and gain in your life. Look with care to know whether it is wealth and possessions you require for your well-being, or rather self-rule and the growth of a will.

Another concern of *Fehu* is to conserve what has already been gained. This Rune urges vigilance and continual mindfulness, especially in times of good fortune, for it is then that you are likely to collapse yourself into your success on the one hand, or behave recklessly on the other. Enjoy your good fortune and remember to share it, for the mark of the well-nourished self is the ability and willingness to nourish others.

113

Reversed: There may be considerable frustration in your life if you draw *Fehu Reversed*, a wide range of dispossessions ranging from trivial to severe. You fall short in your efforts, you reach out and miss; you are compelled to stand by and watch helplessly while what you've gained dwindles away. Observe what is happening. Examine these events from an open perspective and ask, "What do I need to learn from this in my life?"

Even if there is occasion for joy, do not let yourself be seduced into mindless joyousness. Reversed, this Rune indicates that doubtful situations are abundant and come in many forms and guises. Here you are being put in touch with the shadow side of possessions. Yet all this is part of coming to be and passing away, and not that which abides. In dealing with the shadow side of *Fehu*, you have an opportunity to recognize where your true nourishment lies.

Joy
Light

This Rune is a fruit-bearing branch. The term of travail is ended and you have come to yourself in some regard. The shift that was due has occurred; now you can freely receive *Wunjo*'s blessings, whether they be in material gain, in your emotional life or in a heightened sense of your own well-being. This is an alchemical moment in which understanding is transmuted from knowledge. The knowledge itself was a necessary but not sufficient condition; now you can rejoice, having been carried across the gap by the Will of Heaven.

Joyousness accompanies new energy, energy blocked before now. Light pierces the clouds and touches the waters just as something lovely emerges from the depths: The soul is illuminated from within, at the meeting place of Heaven and Earth, the meeting of the waters.

There is a new clarity which may call for you to renounce existing plans, ambitions, goals. It is proper

115

and timely for you to do so, for *Wunjo* is a Rune of restoration, of the self properly aligned with the Self.

Reversed: Things are slow in coming to fruition. The process of birth is long and arduous, and fears arise for the safety of the child within. A crisis, a difficult passage, even if brief, is at hand. Consideration and deliberation are called for. Ask yourself whether you possess the virtues of seriousness, sincerity and emptiness; to possess them is to have tranquillity, which is the ground for patience, clarity and perseverance.

Seen in its true light, *everything is a test*. And so, focused in the present, sincere toward others and trusting in your self, know that you cannot fail.

In times of crisis, *Wunjo Reversed* is a useful meditation.

Harvest
Fertile Season
One Year

A Rune of beneficial outcomes, *Jera* applies to any activity or endeavor to which you are committed. Be aware, however, that no quick results can be expected. A span of time is usually involved; hence the key words "One Year," symbolizing a full cycle before the reaping, the harvest or deliverance.

You have prepared the ground and planted the seed. Now you must cultivate with care. To those whose labor has a long season, a long coming to term, *Jera* offers encouragement of success. Know that the outcome is in the keeping of Providence and continue to persevere.

Remember the old story about the farmer who was so eager to assist his crops that he went out at night and tugged on the new shoots. There is no way to push the river; equally you cannot hasten the harvest. Be mindful that patience is essential for the recognition of your own process which, in its season, leads to the harvest of the self.

14

Kano

Opening

Fire

Torch

This is the Rune of Opening and renewed clarity, of dispelling the darkness that has been shrouding some part of your life. You are free now both to receive gifts and to know the joy of non-attached giving.

Kano is the Rune for the morning of activities, for seriousness, clear intent and concentration, all of which are essential at the beginning of any endeavor. One of the thirteen Cycle Runes, the protection offered by *Kano* is this: The more light you have, the better you can see what is trivial and outmoded in your own conditioning.

In relationships, there can now be a mutual opening up which you may trigger and set in motion through your awareness that the light of understanding is once again available to you both.

Recognize that while on the one hand you are limited and dependent, on the other you exist at the perfect center where the harmonious and beneficent forces of the universe merge and radiate. You *are* that center.

Simply put, if you have been operating in the dark, there is now enough light to see that the patient on the operating table is yourself.

⟩ **Reversed**: Expect a darkening of the light in some situation or relationship. A friendship may be dying, a partnership, a marriage, or some aspect of yourself that is no longer appropriate to the person you are now becoming. Reversed, this Rune points to the death of a way of being that is no longer valid and puts you on notice that failure to face up consciously to that death would constitute a loss of opportunity.

Kano Reversed calls for giving up gladly the old and being prepared to live for a time empty. It calls for developing inner stability, and carries the warning not to be seduced by the momentum of old ways while waiting for the new to become illuminated in their proper time.

15
Teiwaz

The Warrior
Tīw, the Sky God

This is the Rune of the Spiritual Warrior. Always the battle of the Spiritual Warrior is with the self. Funding a will through action, yet unattached to outcomes, remaining mindful that all you can really do is stay out of your own way and let the Will of Heaven flow through you—these are among the hallmarks of the Spiritual Warrior.

Embodied in this Rune is the energy of discrimination, the swordlike quality that enables you to cut away the old, the dead, the extraneous. And yet with the Warrior Rune comes certain knowledge that the universe always has the first move. Patience is the virtue of this Rune, and it recalls the words of St. Augustine that *the reward of patience is patience.*

Here, you are asked to look within, to delve down to the foundations of life itself. Only in so doing can you hope to meet the deepest needs of your nature and tap into your most profound resources. The molding of character is at issue when you draw *Teiwaz.*

Associated with this Rune are the sun, masculine energy, the active principle. The urge for conquest is powerful here, especially self-conquest, which is a lifelong pursuit and calls for awareness, single-mindedness and the willingness to undergo your passage with compassion and in total trust.

When this Rune comes in response to a relationship issue, it indicates that the relationship is both timely and providential. The bond is a real one; there is work for you to do together.

If the issue concerns devotion to a cause, an idea or a path of conduct, the Warrior Rune counsels perseverance, although at times the kind of perseverance called for is patience.

A Rune of courage and dedication, in ancient times *Teiwaz* was the glyph that warriors painted on their shields before battle. Now, the same symbol strengthens our resolve to align the self with the Self.

↓ **Reversed**: The danger is that through hasty or ill-timed action, life force leaks out or is spilled away. If an association is short-lived, do not grieve; know that it has fulfilled its span. Matters of trust and confidence are at issue here, and with them the authenticity of your way of being in the world.

Reversed, *Teiwaz* calls for examining your motives carefully. Is it self-conquest with which you are concerned, or are you trying to dominate another? Are you lusting after outcomes, or are you focused on the task for its own sake?

You will find the answers within yourself, not in outside advice. When you consult the Runes, you are consulting the Self, an action appropriate to the Spiritual Warrior.

Berkana

Growth

Rebirth

Birch Tree

Another of the Cycle Runes, *Berkana* represents a form of fertility that fosters growth both symbolically and actually. The growth may occur in affairs of the world, family matters, the relationship of the self to the Self, or to the Divine.

A Rune that leads to blossoming and ripening, *Berkana* is concerned with the flow of beings into their new forms. Its action is gentle, penetrating and pervasive.

What is called for here is to consider your issue with care and awareness. First disperse resistance, then accomplish the work. For this to happen, your will must be clear and controlled, your motives correct. Any dark corners should be cleansed; this must be carried out diligently and sometimes with expert help. Modesty, patience, fairness and generosity are called for here. Once resistance is dispersed, and rectification carried out and soon to hold firm, then through steadfastness and right attitude, the blossoming can occur.

Reversed: Events or, more likely, aspects of character interfere with the growth of new life. You may feel dismay at failing to take right action. But rather than dismay, what is called for here is diligence. Examine what has occurred, your role in it, your needs, the needs of other people. Are you placing your *wants* before the *needs* of others? Strip away until you can identify the obstacles to growth in this situation. Then, penetrating gently, imitate the wind.

You may be required to cultivate the soil once again, yet through correct preparation, growth is assured.

Movement
Progress
The Horse

Ehwaz is a Rune of transit, transition and movement; of physical shifts, new dwelling places, new attitudes or new life. It also signifies movement in the sense of improving or bettering any situation.

There is about this Rune a sense of gradual development and steady progress, with the accompanying notion of slow growth through numerous shifts and changes. This could apply to the growth of a business or to the development of an idea. A relationship may need to undergo changes if it is to live and grow. Moral effort and steadfastness are called for when you draw Movement, another of the Cycle Runes. Let it be said this way: *As I cultivate my own nature, all else follows.*

This Rune's symbol is the horse, and it signifies the bond between horse and rider. Bronze Age artifacts show a horse drawing the sun across the sky. Here, *Ehwaz* is saying, you have progressed far enough to feel a measure of safety in your position.

Now it is time to turn again and face the future reassured, prepared to share the good fortune that comes your way. The sharing is significant since it relates to the sun's power to foster life and illuminate all things with its light.

Reversed: Movement that appears to block. Be certain that what you are doing—or not doing—is timely. There are no missed opportunities. You have simply to recognize that not all possibilities are open to you, that not all opportunities are appropriate. The opportunity at hand may be precisely to avoid action. If you are feeling at a loss, unclear about the need to act, consider what is timely to your nature and remember: *What is yours will come to you.*

Flow
Water
That Which Conducts

Unseen powers are active here, powers that nour-ish, shape and connect. The attributes of this Rune are water, fluidity, the ebb and flow of emotions, careers and relationships. *Laguz* encourages you to immerse yourself in the experience of living without having to evaluate or understand. It speaks to the satisfaction of emotional needs, to the awakening of the intuitive or lunar side of your nature. For while the sun strives for differentiation, the moon draws us toward union and merging.

This Rune often signals a time for cleansing: for revaluing, reorganizing, realigning. A Rune of deep knowing, it may call you to study spiritual matters in readiness for self-transformation. Success now lies in contacting your intuitive wisdom and attuning to your own rhythms. A Rune of the self relating rightly to the Self, *Laguz* signifies what alchemists called the *conjunc-tio* or sacred marriage. In fairy tales, it is the end where the hero and heroine live happily ever after.

⟨J⟩ **Reversed:** A counsel against overreach and excessive striving. Drawing Flow Reversed is a warning against trying to exceed your own strength, or operate beyond the power you have funded to date in your life.

Laguz Reversed often indicates a failure to draw upon the wisdom of instinct. As a result, the intuitive side of your nature may be languishing, leaving you out of balance. What is called for now is to go within, to honor the receptive side of your Warrior Nature.

Disruption
Elemental Power
Hail

Change, freedom, invention and liberation are all attributes of this Rune. Drawing it indicates a pressing need within the psyche to break free from constricting identification with material reality and to experience the world of archetypal mind.

The Rune of elemental disruption, of events that seem to be totally beyond your control, *Hagalaz* has only an upright position, and yet it always operates through reversal. When you draw this Rune, expect disruption, for it is the Great Awakener, although the form the awakening takes may vary. Perhaps you will experience a gradual feeling of coming to your senses, as though you are emerging from a deep sleep. Then again, the onset of power may be such as to rip away the fabric of what you previously knew as your reality, your security, your understanding of yourself, your work, your relationships or beliefs.

Disruption takes many forms: a relationship fails, plans go awry, a source of supply dries up. But do not be dismayed. Whether you created the disruption, or whether it comes from an outside source, you are not without power in this situation. Your inner strength—the will you have funded until now in your life—provides support and guidance at a time when everything you've taken for granted is being challenged.

Another of the Cycle Runes, the term *radical discontinuity* best describes the action of *Hagalaz* at its most forceful. The more severe the disruption in your life, the more significant and timely the requirements for your growth. The universe and your own soul are demanding that you do, indeed, grow.

Journey
Communication
Union, Reunion

This Rune is concerned with communication, with the attunement of something that has two sides, two elements, and with the ultimate union that comes at the end of the journey, when what is above and what is below are united and of one mind.

Inner worth mounts here, and at such a time you are not intended to rely entirely upon your own power. Instead, ask what constitutes right action. Ask through prayer or meditation, through addressing the Witness Self, the Teacher Within. *Once you are clear, you can neutralize your refusal to let right action flow through you.* Not intent on movement, be content to wait; while you wait, keep on removing resistances. As the obstructions give way, all remorse arising from trying to make things happen disappears.

The journey is toward self-healing, self-change and union. You are concerned here with nothing less than unobstructed, perfect union. But the union of Heaven and Earth cannot be forced. Regulate any excesses in your life. Material advantages must not weigh heavily on this journey of the self toward the Self. Stand apart even from like-minded others; the notion of strength in numbers does not apply at such a time, for this part of the journey—the soul's journey—cannot be shared.

Another of the Cycle Runes, *Raido* carries within its form the Rune of Joy, for now the end is in sight. You are no longer burdened by what you've left behind. Heaven above you and Earth below you unite within you to support you on your way.

A simple prayer for the soul's journey is: *I will to will Thy Will.* Such a Prayer of Intention is proper on any occasion, and is particularly appropriate as a preamble to healing.

Reversed: Receiving *Raido Reversed* puts you on notice to be particularly attentive to personal relationships. At this time, ruptures are more likely than reconciliations and effort may be required to keep your good humor. Whatever happens, how you respond is up to you.

The requirements for your growth may totally disrupt what you had intended. Desired outcomes may elude you. And yet what you regard as detours, inconveniences, disruptions, blockages and even failures and deaths, will actually be *rerouting opportunities*, with union and reunion as the only abiding destinations.

Gateway
Place of Non-Action
The God Thor

With a gateway for its symbol, this Rune indicates that there is work to be done both inside and outside yourself. *Thurisaz* represents the frontier between Heaven and the mundane. Arriving here is a recognition of your readiness to contact the numinous, the Divine, to illuminate your experience so that its meaning shines through its form.

Thurisaz is a Rune of non-action. Thus, the gateway is not to be approached and passed through without contemplation. Here you are being confronted with a clear reflection of what is hidden in yourself, what must be exposed and examined before right action can be undertaken. This Rune strengthens your ability to wait. Now is not a time to make decisions. Deep transformational forces are at work in this next-to-last of the Cycle Runes.

Visualize yourself standing before a gateway on a hilltop. Your entire life lies out behind you and below. Before you step through the gateway, pause and review the past: the learning and the joys, the victories and the sorrows—everything it took to bring you here. Observe it all, bless it all, release it all. For it is in letting go of the past that you reclaim your power.

Step through the gateway now.

4 **Reversed**: A quickening of your development is indicated here. Yet even in times of accelerated growth, you will have reason to halt along the way, to reconsider the old, to integrate the new. Take advantage of these halts.

If you are undergoing difficulties, remember: The nature of your passage depends upon the quality of your attitude, the clarity of your intention and the steadfastness of your will. Be certain that you are not suffering over your suffering.

Drawing *Thurisaz Reversed* demands contemplation on your part. Hasty decisions at this time may cause regrets, for the probability is that you will act from weakness, deceive yourself about your motives, and create new problems more severe than those you are attempting to resolve. Impulses must be tempered by thought for correct procedure. *Do not attempt to go beyond where you haven't yet begun.* Be still, collect yourself, and wait on the Will of Heaven.

Breakthrough Transformation Day

Here is the final Rune belonging to the Cycle of Initiation. Drawing *Dagaz* often signals a major shift or breakthrough in the process of self-change, a complete transformation in attitude, a 180-degree turn. For some, the transition is so radical that they are no longer able to live the ordinary life in the ordinary way.

Because the timing is right, the outcome is assured although not, from the present vantage point, predictable. In each life there comes at least one moment which, if recognized and seized, transforms the course of that life forever. Rely, therefore, on radical trust, even though the moment may call for you to leap empty-handed into the void. With this Rune your Warrior Nature reveals itself.

If *Dagaz* is followed by *The Blank Rune,* the magnitude of the transformation might be so great as to portend a death, the successful conclusion to your passage.

A major period of achievement and prosperity is often introduced by this Rune. The darkness is behind you, daylight has come. Nevertheless, you are reminded not to collapse yourself into thoughts for the future or behave recklessly in your new situation. Considerable hard work can be involved in a time of transformation. Undertake to do it joyfully.

Standstill
Withdrawal
Ice

The winter of the spiritual life is upon you. You may find yourself entangled in a situation to whose implications you are, in effect, blind. You may feel powerless to do anything except submit, surrender, even sacrifice some long-cherished desire. Be patient, for this is the period of gestation that precedes a rebirth.

Positive accomplishment is unlikely now. There is a freeze on useful activity, all your plans are on hold. You may be experiencing an unaccustomed drain on your energy and wonder why: A chill wind is reaching you over the ice floes of old outmoded habits.

Trying to hold on can result in shallowness of feeling, a sense of being out of touch with life. Seek to discover what it is you are holding onto that perpetuates this condition and let go. Shed, release, cleanse away the old; doing so will bring on the thaw.

Usually *Isa* requires a sacrifice of the personal,

the "I." At such a time, you cannot hope to rely on help or friendly support. And yet there is no reason for anxiety. Submit and be still, for what you are experiencing is not necessarily the result of your actions or habits, but rather arises from conditions about which you can do nothing. What has been full must empty, what has increased must decrease. This is the way of Heaven and Earth. To surrender is to display courage and wisdom.

And yet there is another face to Standstill. Just as winter is a time for going within, drawing *Isa* can announce a time of restoration and renewal at the deepest level. In your solitude, exercise caution and do not stubbornly persist in attempting to work your will. Remain mindful that the seed of the new is present in the shell of the old, the seed of unrealized potential, the seed of the good. Trust your own process, and watch for signs of spring.

Wholeness

Life Force

The Sun's Energy

Sowelu stands for wholeness, that which our nature requires. It embodies the impulse toward self-realization and indicates the path you must follow, not from ulterior motives but from the core of your individuality.

Seeking after wholeness is the Spiritual Warrior's quest. And yet what you are striving to become in actuality is what, by nature, you already are. Become conscious of your essence and bring it into form, express it in a creative way. A Rune of great power, making life force available to you, *Sowelu* marks a time for regeneration down to the cellular level.

Although this Rune has no Reversed position, there is reason for caution. You may see fit to withdraw, or even to retreat in the face of a pressing situation, especially if events or people are demanding that you expend your energy now. Know that such a retreat is a retreat in strength, a voyage inward for centering, for balance. Timely retreat is among the skills of the Spiritual Warrior.

Sowelu counsels opening yourself up, letting the light into a part of your life that has been secret, shut away. To accomplish this may call for a profound recognition, for admitting to yourself something that you have long denied.

There is a prayer, known as the *Gayatri*, that embodies the spirit of the Rune of Wholeness. Address the sun in this fashion:

> *You who are the source of all power,*
> *Whose rays illuminate the world,*
> *Illuminate also my heart*
> *So that it too can do Your work.*

While reciting the *Gayatri*, visualize the sun's rays streaming forth into the world, entering your heart, then streaming out from your heart's center and back into the world. This is a powerful and life-enhancing prayer.

There is a caution here not to give yourself airs. Even in a time of bountiful energy you are required to face and vanquish your refusal to let right action flow through you. Nourish this capacity, for it is a mark of true humility.

Practice the art of doing without doing: Aim yourself truly and then maintain your aim without manipulative effort. Meditate on Christ's words: *I can of mine own self do nothing* (John 5:30). For by our own power we do nothing: Even in loving, it is Love that loves through us. This way of thinking and being integrates new energies and permits us to flow into wholeness, which is the ultimate goal of the Spiritual Warrior.

The Unknowable
The Divine
Odin, the All-Father

Blank is the end, blank the beginning. This is the Rune of total trust and should be taken as exciting evidence of your most immediate contact with your own true destiny which, time and again, rises like the phoenix from the ashes of what we call fate.

The appearance of this Rune can portend a death. But that death is usually symbolic and may relate to any part of your life as you are living it now. *Relinquishing control is the ultimate challenge for the Spiritual Warrior.*

Here the Unknowable informs you that It is in motion in your life. In that blankness is held undiluted potential. At the same time both pregnant and empty, this Rune comprehends the totality of being, all that is to be actualized.

Drawing *The Blank Rune* may bring to the surface our deepest fears: Will I fail? Will I be abandoned? Will it all be taken away? And yet our highest good, our truest possibilities and all our fertile dreams are held within that blankness.

Willingness and permitting are what this Rune requires, for how can you exercise control over what is not yet in form? The *Blank Rune* often calls for no less an act of courage than an empty-handed leap into the void. Drawing it is a direct test of faith.

The Unknowable represents the path of *karma*— the sum total of your actions and their consequences, the lessons that are yours for this lifetime. And yet this Rune teaches that the very debts of old karma shift and evolve as you shift and evolve. *Nothing is predestined*: What beckons is the creative power of the unknown.

Whenever you draw *The Blank Rune*, take heart: Know that the work of self-change is progressing in your life.

LOOKING INWARD

I no longer try to change outer things. They are simply a reflection. I change my inner perception and the outer reveals the beauty so long obscured by my own attitude. I concentrate on my inner vision and find my outer view transformed. I find myself attuned to the grandeur of life and in unison with the perfect order of the universe.

—*Daily Word*

Warrior horseman, Mjoboro,
Uppland, Sweden, sixth century

THEATER
OF THE SELF

We are all teachers, and what we teach is what we need to learn, and so we teach it over and over again until we learn it.

—*A Course in Miracles*

Almost five months after establishing the order and meaning of the Runes, while driving south along California's Pacific Coast Highway, I had a strong feeling about their interrelated sequence. I suddenly understood that each Rune is linked to the next through a progressive development which represents the twenty-five steps on the path of the self growing into wholeness.

Without bothering to pull off the road, I opened my notebook and, starting with *Mannaz* ᛗ , the Rune of the Self, jotted down the essential meaning for each Rune as it connected to its neighbor. I wrote steadily as I drove, still in the fast lane, using the steering wheel for support while glancing between the page and the highway. The miles passed by and all the connections flowed into place. I was just coming to the Blank Rune when I caught a movement out of my right eye. Beyond the car window and staring at me with an expression that said, "I don't believe this!" was a highway patrolman on his motorcycle. My speedometer registered 72 mph. He signaled to me to pull over. I didn't even try to explain.

Parked at the roadside, I completed my notes. When I returned home I recopied what I had written, observing its pattern, listening to its rhythm. Not only did the progression hold, it fell into five clusters or acts. Here then are the Viking Runes, divided into Five Acts, in the play of the self coming into alignment with the Self.

Act I: The starting point is the *Self* ᛗ, which, in its willingness to change, undertakes *Partnership* ᚷ at the highest level—partnership with the Divine—and in so doing receives the gift of freedom. The self is assisted in its urge to grow by the Rune of *Signals* ᚠ, which connects the self to the Divine through messages that lead us into to new pathways. During this process, there occurs a retreat, a *Separation* ᚱ which brings about a peeling away of old habits, a shedding of old skins. Once this transformation is under way, *Strength* ᚢ becomes available for loosening the bonds the self has inherited from being in the world. From this strength comes renewed growth into manhood and womanhood.

Act II: This is the moment of *Initiation* ⟨ᚲ⟩, when releasing the old leads to new wholeness. This release occurs on an inner level, for nothing external matters here. Next, the self undergoes the pain of necessary *Constraint* ⟨ᚾ⟩ in order to be cleansed and healed, for rectification always precedes progress. Out of the cleansing comes a new beginning, new creativity and *Fertility* ⟨ᛜ⟩. Since the self is now totally vulnerable, *Defense* ⟨ᛇ⟩ is required. Through being tested, the self develops the power to avert blockage and defeat. This Rune is followed by another more positive form of *Protection* ⟨ᛉ⟩, which calls for correct conduct and timely action: To act appropriately is the self's best protection.

Act III: Now the self can receive the nourishment it requires, either in the form of *Possessions* ⟨ᚠ⟩ or through the achievement of well-being and self-rule. The growth of a will brings *Joy* ⟨ᚹ⟩ from within and a sense of the self properly aligned to the Self. There follows a period of waiting for the *Harvest* ⟨ᛃ⟩, a time marked by patience and perseverance, a time of careful cultivation. Then, with the harvest, the self experiences an *Opening* ⟨ᚲ⟩, more light by which to know the joy of giving. This new light reveals the birth of the *Spiritual Warrior* ⟨ᛏ⟩, the one who possesses the sword of discrimination with which to cut away aspects of the old outgrown life. With the birth of the Spiritual Warrior, the self arrives at the Third Act curtain, the midpoint of the journey.

Act IV: As the Spiritual Warrior pursues the path with a heart, *Growth* [B] is the main concern. There is no urge to turn back. The self is more centered, better prepared when the Rune of *Movement* [M] brings changes and progress: As we cultivate our own nature, all else follows. Aided by the water element *Flow* [I], another cleansing and balancing occurs. Now the self is prepared to face *Disruption* [H] as old outmoded habits fall away. The self acquires new vision as it progresses on its *Journey* [R] toward union with the Divine.

Act V: The path stretches upward, climbing to a *Gateway* [P], a place of non-action that calls for meditation on the progress thus far. Integration is the hallmark of this second stage of initiation. For beyond the Gateway lies a major transformation, a *Breakthrough* [M], signified by radical trust, a leap of faith. Then everything comes to halt, a *Standstill* [I]. Out of that solitary place, life force and the power of *Wholeness* [S] liberate new energies, energies that support a new way of being. Finally, the Spiritual Warrior arrives at the place of The Unknowable, symbolized by *The Blank Rune* [ ], in whose emptiness is found eternal renewal, the starting point for the self.

At the end of Act V, having entered the presence of the Divine, the self is once again at the beginning. *In the life of the spirit, you are always at the beginning.*

THE GIFT OF THE SELF

There are no more maps, no more creeds, no more philosophies. From here on in, the directions come straight from the Divine. The curriculum is being revealed millisecond by millisecond—invisibly, intuitively, spontaneously, lovingly. As one of Thomas Merton's monks has it, "Go into your cell and your cell will teach you everything there is to know." Your cell. Yourself.

—Akshara Noor

Stone lion with runic graffiti, Piraeus, Greece

10

AFTERWORD: MAGIC IN THE PRESENT TENSE

God is alive, magic is afoot.

—Leonard Cohen

At our best, each of us is a channel through which Divine wisdom flows, and we are sensitive to the inner guidance that provides us with the intuitive knowing we require. But life can be hard and difficult and we are not always clear. The channels that we are become blocked by fears, silted up with self-doubt. We do not always hear the still small voice that is our natural inheritance.

The Runes are available to be used as a bridge to your Knowing Self. While contemplating a Rune chosen to illuminate a particular issue, remain clear about one thing: *You are not depending on the Oracle to solve your problems for you.* Images and thoughts will come to mind, image-ideas that will provide you with the necessary clues as to what constitutes timely right action. Working with the Oracle in this way, you will fund a new sense of confidence, a new kind of courage.

The Viking Runes are a mirror for the magic of

our Knowing Selves. In time, as you become skilled in their use, you can lay the Runes aside and permit the knowing to arise unfiltered, just as some dowsers use their bare hands to find water.

Any Oracle is a reflection of the culture in which it evolves. The roots of the Tarot and the *I Ching* are not Western roots. The Tarot did not emerge into Western life until the Runes were more than a thousand years old; the *I Ching* took another eight hundred years to reach the West. In the Runes we are provided with an Oracle that has evolved from the matrix of Western thought. It is both timely and providential that the Viking Runes once again be restored to service as a contemporary Oracle.

To all of you who have arrived at this place of terminations and new beginnings, *Gud blessi thig*.

Bronze girdle ornament
Birka, Sweden, ninth century

SELECTED BIBLIOGRAPHY

The following bibliography, while including few primary sources and far from exhaustive, is intended for those who wish to go more deeply into runic and related studies. Certain books listed (such as those by Loyn, Flowers and Elliott) contain more extensive and scholarly bibliographies.

Anonymous. *Meditations on the Tarot: A Journey Into Christian Hermeticism.* Amity, New York: Amity House, 1985.

Atwater, P.M.H. *The Magical Language of Runes*, Santa Fe, N.M.: Bear & Company, 1992.

Badenoch, Lindsay. *The Daughter of the Runes*. London: Arkana, 1988.

Bates, Brian. *The Way of Wyrd*. London: Century Publishing, 1983.

Beaman, Donald G. *Rune Ryngs*. Boston: Privately Printed, 1988.

Blum, Ralph. *The Book of RuneCards*. New York: St. Martin's Press, 1989

_____. *Rune Play*. New York: Oracle Books, St. Martin's Press, 1985.

Branston, B. *The Lost Gods of England*. London: Thames and Hudson, 1957.

Chadwick, H. M. *The Cult of Othin*. London: Clay and Sons, 1899.

Cooper, D. Jason. *Using the Runes: A Comprehensive Introduction to the Art of Runecraft*. London: Aquarian/Thorsons, 1990.

Dickens, Bruce. *Runic and Heroic Poems of the Old Teutonic Peoples*. Cambridge: Cambridge University Press, 1915.

_____. "Runic Rings and Old English Charms." *Archiv Stud. neuren Sprachen*, vol. 167, 1935.

Dolphin, Deon. *Rune Magic: The Celtic Runes as a Tool for Personal Transformation*. North Hollywood, Calif.: Newcastle, 1987.

Dumezil, Georges. *Gods of the Ancient Northmen*. Edited by Einer Haugen. Berkeley, Calif.: University of California Press, 1973.

_____. *The Destiny of the Warrior*. Translated by A. Hiltebeitel. Chicago: University of Chicago Press, 1973.

Elliot, Ralph W. V. *Runes: An Introduction*. Manchester: Manchester University Press, 1959. (Revised 1989)

_____. "Runes, Yews, and Magic." *Speculum*, vol. 32, 1957.

Ellis, Hilda R. *The Road to Hel.* Cambridge: Cambridge University Press, 1943.

Ellis Davidson, Hilda R. *Gods and Myths of Northern Europe.* London: Penguin, 1946.

Flowers, Stephen E. *Runes and Magic: Magical Formulaic Elements in the Older Runic Tradition.* New York: Peter Lang, 1986.

Franz, Marie-Louise von. *On Divination and Synchronicity: The Psychology of Meaningful Chance.* Toronto: Inner City Books, 1980.

Graham-Campbell, James. *Viking Artefacts, A Select Catalogue.* London: British Museum Publications Limited, 1980.

Grattan, J.H.G., and Singer, S. *Anglo-Saxon Magic and Medicine.* London, 1952.

Halsall, Maureen. *The Old English Rune Poem: A Critical Edition* (McMaster Old English Studies and Texts 2). Toronto: University of Toronto Press, 1981.

Haugen, Einar. *The Scandinavian Languages.* Cambridge, Mass.: Harvard University Press, 1976.

Hermannsson, H. Catalogue of Runic Literature—Part of the Icelandic Collection Bequeathed by Willard Fiske. Cornell University Library.

Hollander, Lee M. *The Poetic Edda.* Austin: University of Texas Press, 1964.

Holmzvist, Wilhem. *Swedish Vikings on Helgo and Birka.* Stockholm: Swedish Booksellers Association, 1979.

Howard, Michael. *The Magic of the Runes.* New York: Samuel Weiser, 1980.

_____. *The Runes and Other Magical Alphabets.* Wellingborough, Northants, England: Aquarian Press, 1978.

Jansson, Sven B. F. *The Runes of Sweden.* Translated by Peter Foote. London: Phoenix House, 1962.

Jones, Gwyn. *History of the Vikings.* London: Oxford University Press, 1968.

Jung, Carl G. *Synchronicity: An Acausal Connecting Principle.* Princeton, N.J.: Princeton University Press, 1973.

154

Knoop, Douglas, and Jones, G. P. *The Mediaeval Mason*. Manchester: Manchester University Press, 1967.

Koestler, Arthur. *The Roots of Coincidence*. London: Hutchinson & Co. Ltd., 1972.

Krause, Wolfgang. *Was Mann in Runen Ritzte*. Halle, Germany: M. Niemeyer, 1935.

Line, David and Julia. *Fortune-Telling by Runes*. Wellingborough, England: Aquarian Press, 1984.

Lowe, Michael, and Carmen Blacker. *Oracles and Divination*. Boulder, Col: Shambhala, 1981.

Loyn, H. R., *The Vikings in Britain*. New York: St. Martin's Press, 1977.

Magnusson, Magnus. *Hammer of the North*. London: Orbis Publishing Limited, 1979.

_____. *Viking Expansion Westwards*. London: Bodley Head Ltd., 1973.

Mattingly, H., *Tacitus: On Britain and Germany*. Harmondsworth, England: Penguin Classics, 1948.

Mercer, Beryl, and Tricia Bramwell. *The Anglo-Saxon Runes*. Amber, England: Phoenix Runes, 1983.

Musset, L. *Introduction á la runologie*. Paris, 1965.

Napier, A. S. "The Franks Casket." *An English Miscellany Presented to Dr. Furnhall*. London: Oxford University Press, 1901.

Osborn, Marijane, and Stella Longland. *Rune Games*. London: Routledge & Kegan Paul, Ltd., 1982.

Page, R. I. *An Introduction to English Runes*. London: Methuen, 1973.

_____. "Anglo-Saxons, Runes, and Magic." *Journal of the Archeological Association* 27: 14–31.

Palsson, Hermann, and Paul Edwards, trans. *Egil's Saga*. England: Penguin, 1976.

Simpson, Jacqueline. *The Viking World*. New York: St. Martin's Press, 1980.

Spiesberger, Karl. *Runenmagie, Handbuch der Runenkunde*. Berlin: Richard Schikowski, 1955.

Stephens, G. *Handbook of the Old-Northern Runic Monuments of Scandinavia and England*. London and Copenhagen, 1884.

_____. *The Old-Northern Runic Monuments of Scandinavia and England*. London and Copenhagen, 1866–1901.

Storms, G. *Anglo-Saxon Magic*. The Hague, 1948.

Syverson, Earl. *Norse Runic Inscriptions with their Long-Forgotten Cryptography*. Sebastopol, Calif., 1979.

Taylor, I. *Greeks and Goths: A Study on the Runes*. London, 1879.

Thompson, Claiborne W. *Studies in Upplandic Runography*. Austin: University of Texas Press, 1975.

Thorsson, Edred. *Futhark: A Handbook of Rune Magic*. York Beach, Maine: Samuel Weiser, 1984.

_____. *Runelore: A Handbook of Esoteric Runology*. York Beach, Maine: Samuel Weiser, 1987.

_____. *At the Well of Wyrd: A Handbook of Runic Divination*. York Beach, Maine: Samuel Weiser, 1988.

Turville-Petre, G., *Myth and Religion of the North*. London: Weidenfeld and Nicholson, 1964.

Urdiz, Gebu. *Magia delle Rune*. Rome: Edizioni Mediterranee, 1977.

Walgren, Erik. *The Kensington Rune Stone: A Mystery Solved*. Madison: University of Wisconsin Press, 1958.

Willis, Tony. *Runic Workbook*. Wellingborough, England: Aquarian Press, 1986.

Wilson, David. *The Vikings and Their Origins*. London: Thames and Hudson Limited, 1970.

Wilson, D. M., and P.G. Foote. *Viking Achievement*. London: Sidgwick and Jackson, 1971.

_____. and Klindt-Jensen, O., *Viking Art*. London: Allen and Unwin, 1966.

PRONUNCIATION GUIDE

GERMANIC		MODERN ENGLISH SOUND VALUE
1. *Mannaz*	män-näz	*a* as in father
2. *Gebo*	gāy-bō	*e* as in play, *o* as in go
3. *Ansuz*	än-sōoz	*a* as in father, *u* as in ooze
4. *Othila*	ō-thē-lä	*o* as in go, *th* as in thin, *i* as in meet, *a* as in father
5. *Uruz*	ōo-rōoz	*u* as in ooze
6. *Perth*	perth	*e* as in berth
7. *Nauthiz*	now-thiz	*au* as in now, *th* as in thin, *i* as in is
8. *Inguz*	ing-gōoz	*ing* as in spring, *u* as in ooze
9. *Eihwaz*	ā-wäz	*ei* as in play, *a* as in father
10. *Algiz*	äl-gēz	*a* as in father, *g* as in gem, *i* as in meet
11. *Fehu*	fā-hew	*e* as in play, *u* as in hew
12. *Wunjo*	wōonjō	*u* as in wound, *j* as in joy, *o* as in go
13. *Jera*	jer-ä	*j* as in join, *e* as in yes, *a* as in father
14. *Kano*	kä-nō	*a* as in father, *o* as in go
15. *Teiwaz*	tā-wäz	*ei* as in play, *a* as in father

GERMANIC		MODERN ENGLISH SOUND VALUE
16. *Berkana*	ber-kä-nä	*e* as in berry, *a* as in father
17. *Ehwaz*	eh-wäz	*eh* as in yes, *a* as in father
18. *Laguz*	lä-g̅o̅o̅z	*a* as in father, *u̱* as in ooze
19. *Hagalaz*	hä-gä-läz	*a* as in father, *g* as in give
20. *Raido*	rî-thō	*ai* as in ride, *d* as in though, *o* as in go
21. *Thurisaz*	thu-ri-säz	*th* as in thin, *u* as in pull, *i* as in easy, *a* as in father
22. *Dagaz*	thä-gäz	*d* as in that, *a* as in father
23. *Isa*	ē-sä	*i* as in easy, *a* as in father
24. *Sowelu*	sō-wä-l̅o̅o̅	*o* as in go, *e* as in way, *u* as in ooze
25. *Odin*	ō-din	*o* as in go, *i* as in thin

THE RUNEWORKS

Using the Viking Runes has been, for many people, an adventure in self-discovery. We are most interested in hearing of *your* experiences with the Runes. Please feel encouraged to write to us at The Rune-Works.

To this end, we publish *The New Oracle*, a newsletter that serves as a forum for all of us to share our runic experiences. It contains interviews with seminal thinkers of our time, information about other oracular traditions, and innovations in Rune casting techniques discovered by those who use the Oracle. We would like to quote from your letters; if you wish your name withheld, please let us know.

If you have difficulty finding *The Book of Runes*, *Rune Play,* or *The RuneCards*, or prefer to purchase additional copies (with or without stones or cards) directly through us, please mail your inquiries to The RuneWorks.

If you wish to subscribe to *The New Oracle*, receive *The RuneWorks Catalogue*, or be placed on our mailing list for upcoming workshops, please write to:

The RuneWorks
P.O. Box 1320
Venice, CA 90294

We look forward to hearing from you.

Ralph H. Blum

ABOUT THE AUTHOR

Ralph H. Blum received his degree in Russian studies at Harvard. Following a period in Italy as a Fulbright Scholar, he returned to Harvard, where he did graduate work in anthropology with grants from the National Science Foundation and the Ford Foundation.

Encountering the Runes while doing research in England, he subsequently explored their origins and reinterpreted their meanings in terms appropriate for our time. Ralph H. Blum has been working with the Viking Runes as a tool for self-counseling since 1977.

Silver cup from a royal grave.
Jelling, Jutland, Denmark, tenth century

Futhark (*Traditional Order*)

MODERN ENGLISH EQUIVALENT	OLD ENGLISH RUNES	NAMES	GERMANIC RUNES	NAMES	ETRUSCAN	PRE-RUNIC SYMBOLS
f	ᚠ	feoh	ᚠ	fehu		
u	ᚢ	ūr	ᚢ	ūruz		△
þ (th)	ᚦ	þorn	ᚦ	þurisaz		
a	ᚪ	ōs		ansuz	A	
r	ᚱ	rād	ᚱ	raiðō		
k		cēn	<	kaunaz kēnaz kanō		
g	ᚷ	gyfu	ᚷ	gebō		X
w	ᚹ	wyn	ᚹ	wunjō		
h	ᚻ	haegl	ᚺ	hagalaz		ᛂ
n	ᚾ	nȳð	ᚾ	nauþiz		+
i	ᛁ	īs	ᛁ	īsa	ᛁ	ᛁ
j		gēr		jēra		
e (ei)		ēōh		eihwaz		
p		peorð		perþ		
z		eolh-secg		algiz		
s		sigel		sowelu		
t	↑	tīr	↑	teiwaz		
b	ᛒ	beorc	ᛒ	berkana		
e	ᛗ	e(o)h	ᛗ	ehwaz		
m	ᛗ	man	ᛗ	mannaz		
l	ᛚ	lagu	ᛚ	laguz		
ng		Ing	□	inguz		
o	◊	eþel	◊	oþila		
ð	ᛞ	daeg	ᛞ	ðagaz		

Note: While the order of Rune names was to some degree fortuitous, the choice of names was not. A Rune name had to begin with a given sound and possess mnemonic power